MANDY

Chapter One

March, 2014 (Philadelphia)
	Getting robbed at gun point isn't usually a positive life-changing experience, but for me it was.
	It happened at night not long after Mandy and I had moved to Philly from Utah. A guy who'd been following me stepped in front of me and turned to face me. He had his hand in his jacket pocket. "Stink 'em oop," he said in a deep bass voice.
	He was taller than me and was wearing a beat-up coat with the collar up.
	"Sorry. I didn't understand what you said. Could you say it again?"
	"Stink 'em oop! Stink 'em oop!" He pulled his hand out of his jacket so I could see his gun. "Give me you moaney."
	During my mission, headquartered in New York City, our mission president had often told us what to do if we were ever held up. His counsel was to stay calm and be cooperative. "Give them whatever they want. It's only money. We can replace that, but we can't replace you."
	"Oh, I get it. This is a stick up, right? That's why you have the gun, right?"
	He nodded.
	"Is it okay if I get my wallet? It's in my pocket."
	He nodded. "All you moaney."
	The verse from Mandy's song came into my mind:

My Lord He has no throwaways.
There's no one He don't love.
All the folks you see today
Are loved by Him above.

	Oh yeah? I thought. *Well this guy is definitely a throwaway.*
	But then another thought popped into my mind. *Is there anything about him that would make him not a throwaway?*
	"I don't have much money, but you can have all I've got. Oh, I have a bus pass here too."
	He had been trying to talk softly but I'd made him mad so now his voice rang out. "No pass! Just moaney!"

Well, his voice for one thing. It's got a lot of overtones.

I started looking through my wallet. "Okay, I got a ten-dollar bill here. You can have that."

"All you moaney!"

I handed him my wallet. "Look through this. Take anything you want. Oh, I've got a watch here too if you'd like that. Also, I'll be getting some money on Friday if you want to come back then."

He didn't find anything in my wallet and handed it back.

"What about my watch?"

He sighed and shook his head. "Just moaney."

"Well, then, and I know this will seem like a strange thing for me to ask, but by any chance, do you like to sing?"

He pulled the gun out of his pocket again and pointed it at me. "You want me shoot you? Is that you want?"

"No. I just want to know if you can sing. Because you could make much money if you can sing."

"You crazy man!"

"Okay, look, because of how deep your voice is, it's possible you could be making like two hundred dollars a day if you can sing. Without the gun."

"That crazy talk!"

"Not really. Let's see what you got."

"I got gun!"

"I know but I just want to know if you can sing."

He shook his head. "You crazy man."

"I know. Okay, I'm going to sing part of a song and then I want you to sing it with me. Okay?"

He put his gun back into his pocket.

Now all I had to do was to get him to sing.

     *   *   *

<u>August, 2012 (Provo, Utah)</u>

One month after getting back from my mission, I began my sophomore year at BYU. After the first day of class, I went to my campus ward's opening social, held at Canyon Glen Park in Provo Canyon. After visiting with my new bishop, I looked around and tried to decide which girl I'd most like to meet.

I soon had my winner. It was the girl wearing her favorite sweatshirt. I knew it was her favorite because it was a faded orange and had a small rip in the right sleeve. You got to be totally self-confident to wear that to a ward opening social. Her reddish-brown hair was in a ponytail, like she had more important things to do than fuss over herself. Also, she was the only girl wearing beat-up hiking boots, like she didn't really care what people thought, or that there were more important things in life than hoping that some random guy like me might want to get to know her better.

Even with all that downplaying, she was still amazingly beautiful. That was even more impressive to me because it seemed like she didn't have to work at it.

As I approached her, she was talking to another girl in the ward. "Hi, are you two new in the ward?" I asked.

She scowled. "No, but you are."

"Yes I am. I'm David. I just got off a mission in New York City. You know, the Big Apple?"

She shook her head. "The Big Apple?" And then they both smirked.

Even though this wasn't going well, I wasn't disappointed. Having spent hundreds of hours trying to talk to people going to and from subways in NYC had taught me to never give up. "What are your names?" I asked.

"I'm Mandy and this is my roommate Sara."

"Great to meet you both," I said. My guess was that Sara had chosen her white plastic-frame glasses because she thought they made her look smart. That might have been true, but the downside was that she ran the risk of being referred to by guys in the ward as "you know, that chick with the white glasses."

Sara had long dark brown hair. She was wearing a BYU T-shirt which I could tell was new because it still had the creases where it had been folded in the factory.

"You know what? I bet you're really hungry," Mandy said. "Why don't you go get something to eat? We've got plenty of burgers and hot dogs. A big guy like you could probably down two or three burgers, right?"

"I'll go get something to eat in a minute. What were you two talking about?" I asked.

"I was just talking about my dog Muffy," Sara said.

"What breed?" I asked

"German shepherd."

I burst out laughing. "You named a German Shepherd Muffy? Man, I bet he takes some razzing from the other dogs in the neighborhood!" I did my mission-perfected Brooklyn accent. "Hey, Muffy, ya owna's cawlin! She wants ya to go and have some tea and crumpets."

I started to laugh until I noticed that Sara looked like she was about to cry.

"Sara was just telling me that Muffy recently died," Mandy said.

I cleared my throat. "Sara, look, I am so sorry that your dog Muf..." I wanted to say Muffy but didn't think I'd be able to do that without laughing. "You know...died."

"We won't keep you any longer," Mandy said. "Go meet others in the ward and get something to eat."

"I will. Great to meet you both! Let me say again how sorry I am about your dog's passing. He's in a better place now. You know, like in some kind of... uh...celestial kennel."

That only made Sara cry more.

Mandy scowled at me "Please... just...go," she said slowly and distinctly.

So I left. Okay, it wasn't great but at least I left on a high note.

I introduced myself to a few other girls in the ward, but I wasn't interested in any of them. The ones I met were either in graduate school or else freshmen. So for me they were either too mature or not mature enough.

I noticed a guy on crutches so I went over to talk to him. It's always interesting to find out how someone broke his leg. He had some food stains on his sports shirt which made me think he'd already eaten.

I found out that his name is Zach. He's from Provo. He told me he'd broken his leg turning off the hose in their backyard late at night.

"Hey, c'mon, Man, if you want to impress the girls, you got to come up with a better story than that," I said. "Like you saw this elderly woman being robbed and you went to her rescue, and that's when you fought all four of the thugs and, during the fight, they threw you off a cliff, and that's how you broke your leg. But the good news is that woman got safely away during the fight. How about you start using that story?"

He shook his head. "But that wouldn't be the truth," Zach said.

I cleared my throat. "Well, yeah, that's true. And, actually, Zach, that's a real good point there."

Zach told me that he's majoring in history and hopes to be a college professor someday.

I told him about going to Ellis Island on my mission where people coming into the United States used to have to go, and how I found the name of one of my ancestors who had come through there in the early 1900s. He actually knew a lot about Ellis Island, and what he told me was actually interesting.

Mandy saw us talking and came over. "I see you've met Zach," she said to me.

"Yeah, he's already given me a lesson on the importance of telling the truth and now he's giving me a history lesson."

She smiled. "Zach teaches us all."

Zach got a big smile on his face.

We talked for a while and then Mandy said, "I see we're running out of relish. I'd better get some more."

"Let me help you with that," I said.

"You think I need help getting a bottle of relish?" she asked.

"No, not really, but I like to serve others. I'm a very helpful person."

"What do you think, Zach? Should I let David go with me out to my pickup to get some relish?"

Zach nodded.

"Okay, let's go," she said.

"You're the best, Zach!" I said as we left him.

On our way to the parking lot I again apologized for making fun of Sara's dog.

Mandy shrugged. "Don't worry about it. You didn't know Muffy was dead when you made fun of its name."

"That's true. Thanks."

"No problem. And thanks for being friendly to Zach. Not everyone is."

"Why's that?" I asked.

"He's very smart but he lacks some basic social skills."

"Like me, right?" I said with a smile.

She laughed. "Exactly. By the way, please tell me more about the celestial dog kennel."

"My guess is you haven't done a serious study of The Book of Leviticus, have you? That's where you'll find most of the references to dog kennels in heaven."

She smirked at me. "How interesting! Can you give me the chapter and verse?"

"Uh, not right now. It's in my scripture journal though."

She shook her head. "Yes, I'm sure it is."

She drove a late model Ford pickup. She retrieved a jar of relish from the floor of the front seat.

"Here, let me carry that for you," I said.

"Why?"

"Because I am so strong and manly that a bottle of relish is no challenge for me."

"You sure about that?" she teased. And then she laughed, which caused a dimple on her right cheek to appear. It was like her gift to anyone who made her happy.

"Please let me carry the relish. I just got off my mission, so serving others is very important to me."

She handed me the relish. "Well, okay, give it a shot. But, look, if it's too heavy for you, just let me know." I loved her smile.

I picked it up like it was only a jar of relish, which of course, it was.

"You are so strong!" she mocked.

I nodded. "You know what? I could carry a couple of these at a time with no problem."

"Hard to believe," she said with a grin.

As we started back, she glanced up at the mountains around us and then sighed.

"You okay?" I asked.

"It's just that it's hard to be up here and not be hiking."

"Let's go on a hike then. Don't' worry. I'll protect you from the bears."

She smiled. "What bears?"

"Are you kidding me? The woods here are full of bears."

"I haven't seen any signs warning people about bears."

"That's because the bears here are so aggressive they tear down all the signs."

She laughed. "You're talking about the bears being aggressive, right?"

"Okay, look. Whatever awkward moments you and I have had since meeting can be blamed on me having served a mission in New York City where being self-assertive was valued. Also, on my mission, I was surrounded by elders who appreciated my warped sense of humor. Let me also say that you're the first girl I've tried to flirt with for over two years. So, obviously, I'll get better with practice."

"We can only hope so," she said with a smile.

"How about that hike?" I asked.

She glanced at my flip-flops. "As a certified wilderness guide, let me say that you are not prepared to go on a hike. Excuse me. I need to take the relish to the table." She took the bottle away from me.

"You're no wilderness guide!" I called out to her when she was about ten feet from where she'd left me.

She turned to face me. "Am too." And then she left.

I went to my car and fished out an old pair of hiking boots, grabbed a beat-up cowboy hat that used to be my dad's, and waited for her to be alone again.

I approached her and said. "Hey, Girl, go take a hike! With me, okay?"

She checked out my hiking boots and hat. "All right, you're on, but we'll have to come back in a few minutes."

"Why's that?" I asked.

"Because I need to welcome everyone."

Being a vocal music major, it was easy to get people's attention. "Excuse me, everyone! On behalf of the activities committee, Mandy and I want to welcome you all to the ward opening social. At this time Mandy will say a few words of welcome."

Mandy gave a standard welcome to the ward, asked for someone to say a prayer and then introduced the bishop, who said a few words of welcome. When he was done, she walked over to me. "Okay, let's go. But before we go, I need to tell you something."

"Okay."

"I don't do leisurely hikes," she said. "So if you want to preserve whatever shred of male pride you may still have after your disastrous Muffy conversation, this might be a good time to back out gracefully."

"Yeah, right," I muttered.

"I'm serious. If you can't keep up, it's okay. I'll totally understand. I've never met a guy yet who can keep up with me on the trail."

I laughed. "I'm sure that won't be a problem for me."

She smiled and shook her head. "Really? Well, let's find out. Also, if the only reason you want to take a hike with me is because you're hoping to get to know me better, you can forget about that too because you'll be so out of breath that you won't be able to speak and, even if you could, I'll be so far away I won't hear anything you say."

"I seriously doubt that."

She shook her head. "On your mission in New York, you must have faced rejection every day right?"

I sighed. "Yeah, but hey, don't feel sorry for me."

"I don't, but I'm guessing that as a way to avoid being depressed all the time you made up little fantasies in your head that this'd be the day you'd have great success. But most days that didn't happen, did it?"

"Why are you bringing this up?" I asked.

"Because this hike with me will be a lot like that for you."

I scoffed. "I doubt that."

"Always the optimist, right? Well, that's good but sometimes you have to face reality. And, sadly, this will be one of those times. The only reason I'm even talking to you now is because you made an effort to make friends with Zach. So we'll go but don't say I didn't warn you. But first, give me a minute. I've got to get something from my rig." She ran back to her pickup, grabbed a waist-pack, fastened it around her and returned.

And then we started up the trail. She went easy on me for a couple of minutes and then she said, "Okay, let's pick up the pace just a little, okay?"

"Yeah, sure. This is way too slow for me."

"Really?" she asked. And then she took off up the trail. I had to run just to keep up with her. She'd look back occasionally to see if I'd dropped out yet. My muscles were aching and I was out of breath but I refused to quit.

The only reason she eventually stopped was because we ran out of mountain. Near the summit we stopped. She came up to me and gave me a high five. "Way to keep up!"

"Thanks."

She turned to face an outcropping of rock about twenty feet up from where we were. "What would you think about us going up there?" she asked.

"Yeah, sure, no problem."

"Do you know how to rock climb?" she asked.

"Not really. Do you?"

"Of course."

"Just go ahead of me, give me a few hints, and I'll just do what I see you doing."

"Are you sure? If you fall, it will be certain death."

"So, I won't fall."

"Okay then, let's go."

The only way I made it to the top was by doing exactly what she told me to do.

On a ledge near the top we sat down to rest. Because it was not a very long ledge, we ended up next to each other with our shoulders touching. I was okay with that.

"You made it!" she said. "I'm impressed! You didn't give up and you didn't complain."

"I was too scared to complain," I joked.

She grabbed two granola bars and a small bottle of water from her waist-pack. She gave me one of the granola bars and then took the other. We sat in silence and chewed. And then she opened the water and let me have the first drink. I drank about half and then handed it back to her. She took the bottom of her sweatshirt and used it to wipe off the top, then took a big swig.

"Tell me about yourself," I said.

"What do you want to know?"

"How you got to be the way you are now."

She paused. "Actually, I'm not sure I'd feel comfortable telling that to someone I just met."

I shrugged. "Whatever you want to tell me will be great."

"Well, one thing I can tell you is that I have a horse named Dance-A-Lot. Since I was twelve he's been my best friend. Back then, some nights in the summer, I slept in the barn with him."

"You slept in a barn?" I asked. "Was your mom okay with that?"

She looked down, brought her hand up to shield her face, and sighed.

"You okay?" I asked.

"Not really."

"Did I say something wrong?" I asked.

"I don't normally talk about this with strangers, but…" She sighed. "My mom died when I was eleven," she said softly.

"Oh, I'm so sorry to hear that."

"Thank you," she said. "My dad and I were both devastated. He quit his job as a corporate lawyer in California. We drove to Wyoming. His plan was to stop at the first small town with good scenery and a lake nearby. That turned out to be Pinedale, Wyoming. My dad sold our home in California and bought a house on a five-acre lot a few miles from town. That's when he bought me Dance-A-Lot." She paused. "I don't know why I'm even telling you this."

I patted her on the arm. "I'm so sorry about your mom."

"Thank you."

I sighed. "Actually, I know a little about what you went through. My dad died when I was nine."

"I'm very sorry you've gone through this too."

"Thanks." I sighed. "Everyone's sorry. For all the good that does, right?"

"I know what you're saying," she said.

"How did you and your dad deal with this?" I asked.

"The next summer, because of some of my dad's friends in our ward, and also his business connections in California, he became a guide, taking business men with more money than sense into the mountains for hunting, fishing or just enjoying nature."

"What did he do with you when he was gone?" I asked.

"He took me with him. At first I just sat around and complained. But then he hired me to help out. In time I began to develop a certain sense of pride in all the skills I was acquiring. And, also, I came to love the outdoors."

"So that's where your Ninja hiking comes from?" I asked.

"Yeah."

"I went on a fifty-mile hike once," I said.

She smiled. "Just once?"

I nodded. "I pretty much learned everything I needed to learn on just that one hike."

"And what was that?" she asked.

"Never do that again."

She smiled. "For me being outdoors is the only time I really feel alive."

"Did you and your dad do the mountain guide thing this summer?" I asked.

"Just during July. He's not doing it as much now." She took another drink of water. "I guess he'd still be doing it if he weren't such a big mouth. When it came to issues about legal matters, he started showing up at meetings and asking a lot of questions. The questions were so good that before we knew it, he'd been appointed state attorney general by the governor. That meant we had to move to Cheyenne, the state capitol. We moved when I was fifteen. At first I didn't like it there. I even got in a few fights with some girls who thought they were better than me, and when my dad heard about it, he got mad and told me I needed to learn to be more of a lady, so he made me take piano lessons and sing in the school choir."

"So you can sing?" I asked hopefully.

"Yeah, except my choir teacher had to keep telling me to sing quieter because I was drowning out all the other girls."

"That wasn't your fault. The other girls should have sung louder," I said.

She rummaged through her pack. "I thought of telling her that but I was already labeled as a trouble maker so I tried to blend in more with the other girls. I got some trail mix here too. You want some?"

"Yeah, that'd be great. Tell me more about yourself."

She poured some trail mix in my hand. "In school I got into soccer, basketball, and track. And so, when it came time to go to college, it was natural for me to pick P.E. as a major."

I tilted my head back and let the trail mix pour into my mouth. "After watching you run up the trail, I can believe that."

She smiled. "I kept expecting you to quit. But you never did."

"No."

"How come?" she asked.

"I was trying to prove to you that you should let me be your friend."

"Why?"

I wasn't sure how she'd take this. "Well, because you intrigue me."

She seemed surprised. "Why's that?"

"You're such an amazing mixture of things," I said.

"In what way?"

"You're awesome looking but you show up in a sweatshirt with a tear in the sleeve and old hiking boots and your hair in a pony tail that my guess is that you spent at most thirty seconds on. It's like you don't care what guys think about you. You don't seem needful of anything."

"Actually I am very self-reliant. Give me a knife and I could survive in the mountains for a year," she said.

I shrugged. "So what you're saying is that you couldn't do it without the knife, right?"

In slow motion she faked trying to push me off the cliff. "And what would you need to survive a year?"

"Just one credit card," I said with a big smile.

That got her laughing. *Does she have any idea what affect her dimple has on the people around her?* I thought. *It makes me want to get her to laugh or smile just to be rewarded by it.*

She poured some more trail mix into my cupped hands. My new goal was to take as much time as possible finishing it off in order to be able to spend more time with her. "This tastes good, especially when you're stranded on a cliff," I said.

"We're not stranded. At least I'm not."

"How are we going to get down?" I asked.

"By going up. I'll show you how. Just trust me. But before we go, tell me some more about yourself. How did your dad die?"

"Car accident. Coming home from work."

"I'm so sorry."

I nodded and sighed. "So my mom raised me."

"Where are you from?" she asked.

"San Francisco. It's a great place if you love music and the arts."

"And you do?" she asked.

"My mom does. She got me taking singing and dance lessons."

"Why did you agree to take dance lessons?" she asked.

"My mom wanted me to. Besides, it was good exercise and helped me develop coordination and stamina. I still work out every day. That's why I was able to keep up with you on the trail and then follow you up the cliff."

She smirked. "You'll have to put on a cute little dance for me sometime."

I shook my head. "Probably not. I was just a little guy when I starting dancing. Now I weigh nearly 200 pounds and I'm six foot three. So I'm probably not going to get a part in The Nutcracker Suite unless they want me to help the nutcracker by hunting down and maiming all the mice-men."

She laughed. "That's one performance I'd attend! Do you still sing?"

"Yeah, I do. Actually, I'm majoring in vocal performance in the Music Department. My dream is to someday perform on a regular basis at the Metropolitan Opera in New York City."

"Will you sing for me?" she asked.

"Yeah, sometime."

"I mean now," she said.

"I don't have my music."

"Just sing something you know."

"Why?" I asked.

"Because I want to hear you sing."

"Why?"

"Why did you climb up here with me?" she asked.

"To gain your respect."

She rested her hand on my arm. "You'll totally have my respect if you sing for me now."

"I don't do country-western, okay?"

She pretended to be offended. "You think that's the only kind of music a girl from Wyoming would like?"

"Yeah, pretty much," I teased.

She moved the bag of trail mix away from me. "No more trail mix for you!"

I shrugged. "No big loss. The M&M's are the only things I like from it anyway."

She smiled. "I know. Me too. C'mon, Cowboy, sing for me. I don't care what you sing. Just sing."

"What if you don't like it?" I asked.

She smiled. "Then I'll leave you stranded up here and you'll have to figure out by yourself how to get down."

I smiled. "So there's a lot depending on this, right?"

"Could be." She placed her hand on my forearm. "Please sing for me."

"Okay. This is from the opera *La Bohéme*. I'll be trying out for the lead tomorrow."

I began to sing my part of "Sono andati?", a duet near the end of the opera. At first it seemed strange to be singing outdoors. I wondered what the birds were thinking.

When I finished and turned to her, there were tears on her cheeks. "I listened to this one time in a music appreciation class," she said. "It's about someone dying, isn't it?"

"Yeah, it is."

"I almost never cry anymore about my mom, but what you sang was very beautiful, but also very sad," she said.

"It is sad."

"I still miss my mom so much," she said.

"Of course you do, just like I miss my dad."

"I have so many questions I want to ask her," she said. "Things I never would have thought to ask her when I was eleven. " She sighed. "Sometimes I feel...well, I'm not sure how to explain it... incomplete."

I nodded. "That's the way I feel too because of my dad being gone. But I can't do anything about it. All I can do is move on."

"I know. I don't talk much anymore about my mom," she said. "And even when I try to tell people how much I still miss her, they always say something like 'Well, at least you still have your dad', or the one I hate the most, 'Your mom is in a better place.' Well you know what? It's not better for me. Why can't they just shut up and let me tell them how it feels to lose a parent without trying to shut me up?"

"I've had that happen to me too. Okay, look, even if you can't tell anyone else about what it's been like for you, tell me."

And so she told me all the sad and painful experiences she'd gone through since her mom's death. I just let her talk without trying to stop her or cheer her up. I did try, though, to be supportive in my comments.

When she was done, she wiped her face with her sleeve. "Thank you for listening. I'm sorry for unloading on you," she said.

"I'm glad you felt comfortable enough with me to do that."

"I am too," she said. "Do you want to tell me how it was for you after losing your dad?"

I paused and cleared my throat. "Not now. Maybe someday though."

"Sure, anytime you're ready."

"You think we might actually end up being friends?" I asked.

She nodded. "Maybe so."

"Let's change the subject. Tell me what you like about being in a place like this."

"It's so beautiful. Like that tree over there."

"What about the tree?"

She saw more in one tree than I ever would.

I was actually more interested in her than the tree though, especially the way the sun was highlighting her reddish brown hair. Certain strands were glowing but when she moved her head a little, other strands would light up.

"I see what you mean about the beauty here," I said.

She looked at her watch. "We should go now though. I need to help with clean-up."

"You know what? If I get out of here alive, I'll help you with that," I said.

"That would be great." She touched my arm. "Can I be serious now? Because of you listening to me talk about how it has been for me to have lost my mom, this will always be a special place to me."

"For me too."

"I usually don't talk about my mom," she said.

"I'm the same way. On my mission, my mission president's wife once asked me if I'd sent my dad a Father's Day card. I told her yes because I didn't want to let her know about my dad because then she'd ask how it happened and then I'd talk about it. She'd listen for a minute or two, and then say, 'Sometimes we just need to move on.' People say that a lot."

"That's what they say to me too, and, actually, I don't dwell as much on my mom now." She sighed. "Except on her birthday, and my birthday, and Mother's Day, and Thanksgiving, and Christmas, and New Year's Day, and when I've had a good day, oh, and when I've had a bad day." She sighed. "I sound pathetic, don't I?"

"No, you sound the way anyone would who's lost a parent."

"What about you?"

I sighed. "My dad was always busy and he kept promising to teach me how to play sports." I paused. "But that never happened. A few days before he died he put up a basketball hoop on our garage. He was going to teach me how to play basketball on Saturday of that week, but then he died. Sometimes I wish we'd done that together, you know, at least once." I sighed. "But we never did."

"If you're at all interested, I can teach you how to play basketball," she said.

"That'd be good."

She got to her feet. "Okay, let's go. How this will work is like playing follow the leader with me, of course, being the leader." She flashed me a big grin.

"I won't argue about that until we're off this place."

She climbed up higher until she reached a portion of the mountain that was not so steep.

"Okay, your turn," she said.

She directed me in every move I made until I got to where she was.

She high-fived me. "Way to be! You're a natural climber!"

"I've got a great teacher."

"Now we just hike down until we come to the trail," she said.

"Okay."

When it was wide enough on the trail, we walked side by side. But when it got narrow and steep, she went ahead of me.

When we were farther down the mountain and on an easy trail, she grabbed my cowboy hat off my head and ran away. "You want this? Come and get it!"

I started to chase her through the woods. Being an opera major, I could make my voice sound like a villain. "I am so coming to get you!" I called out, followed by an evil laugh.

"You'll never catch me!" she yelled back.

"I will because I'm the world's fastest human. I'm just playing with you now, to build up your confidence before I totally smoke you."

We came to a clearing in the woods. She stopped and turned to face me. "You want this? Come and get it," she teased, holding out my hat.

I walked slowly toward her. When I was almost close enough to grab my hat, she ran away again, laughing.

Naturally I ran after her. But not fast enough to catch her. This was way too much fun to have it come to an end anytime soon.

And so it went. She was running through the woods laughing. And I was lumbering after her, doing my evil villain imitation.

Good stuff, right?

She stopped again and waited for me to catch up.

I walked slowly toward her. The sun was highlighting her hair and she was grinning at me, which revealed her dimple. "You look real good out here in the woods," I said.

"Thanks. You look good too. You want to know my reaction when I first saw you?" she asked. "You reminded me of a hero in a Disney movie."

"Yeah, that sounds about right, but which hero?"

"I can't remember his name but he was tall, handsome, had a narrow waist, good posture, and a great voice."

"Check, check, check, check, and check. Yeah, that's me all right."

"Oh, and also, he wasn't very smart." And then with a huge grin, she added, "Check!"

"Girl, you are in so much trouble!"

She started running and laughing while I lumbered after her.

Finally she stopped. "I figured out which movie character you remind me of?"

"Mr. Incredible?" I asked.

With a teasing smile on her face, she said, "No, Winnie the Pooh!"

I threw up my hands. "Winnie the Pooh? Seriously?"

"Wait, I remember now. It wasn't Winnie the Pooh. It was Donald Duck!"

Actually I can do an imitation of how Donald Duck speaks. And so I did.

"Yes, that's perfect!"

We decided to sit down on a big boulder to catch our breath.

"See that tree over there." She picked up a rock. "And see this Bad Boy here? Watch this." She threw the rock at the tree and hit it. "What do you think about that, hey?"

I shrugged. "No big deal."

"What are you talking about? There's no way you can do that."

"Oh, you mean destroy nature? Why would I even want to do that? I am a friend to nature."

She smiled and shook her head. "How are you a friend of nature?"

"I leave it alone and don't go throwing rocks at it like you do."

"Whatever. The pressure's on. Let's see you hit that tree."

"I totally got this." I picked up a flat rock. "See this Bad Girl? Watch what I can do with it."

"Whoa there, Cowboy! It's never a Bad Girl. It's always a Bad Boy."

"Yeah, right." I said sarcastically. I got up, walked over to the tree, and set the rock on one of the limbs and then came back. "There you go."

We had the last of the trail mix, and ended up arguing over the last M&M. Eventually, though, I let her have it.

"I got a question for you," she said. "When you were talking to Zach, you told me that he'd taught you an important lesson about honesty. What was that about?"

I paused. "I asked him how he broke his leg and he told me it happened when he went to turn off the water in his backyard late at night. I told him that if he wanted to impress girls, he needed to come up with a better story than that."

"And did you give him a story?"

"Yeah, I did."

"What was the story you came up with?" she asked.

"That he came across an elderly woman being robbed and he

fought all four thugs but then they threw him off a cliff. And that's how he broke his leg. But the woman was safe and got away."

"So you were suggesting Zach lie in order to impress girls? That's a little worrisome to me."

"I wasn't serious about suggesting Zach lie. I didn't realize he'd take me seriously."

"Have you lied to me since we've met to impress me?"

"No, of course not. And I never will."

She nodded. "Sorry for cross-examining you. That's one of the downsides of having an attorney general for a dad."

We sat down and took a few selfies of us together.

"We look good together," she said as we reviewed the pictures.

"I agree."

We started walking again. When I wasn't looking, she poured what was left of the water over my hat. With both of us laughing, I chased her.

Finally she stopped. "I've never had so much fun before in my life with a guy."

She was standing still, leaning up against the trunk of a big oak tree. I raised my arm and leaned it against the tree over her head. "It has been amazing for me as well. What would you think if we kissed, like one time?" I asked.

She moved away from me. "You can't be serious! We just met," she said. "Why would you even suggest that?"

"Well, it just seems like it would fit in, you know, with all the chasing and the teasing. You know what I mean?" I asked.

"Suppose we get married and someday our teenage daughter asks when we first kissed, and we tell her it was within an hour of meeting each other. Is that a lesson you want your daughter to learn from us?"

"So you're already starting to think about us getting married, right?" I said with a grin on my face because I knew what her reaction would be.

She pulled my hat down over my eyes. "You totally love playing the part of the clueless jerk, don't you?" she asked.

"Yeah, pretty much," I said. "Okay, look, I know this is going to be a big disappointment to you, but I really think we should wait a few days before we kiss."

"A big disappointment to me? You're the one who brought it up!"

"Okay, let me explain. For me to even be thinking about this has got to do with me chasing you. You know, like in third grade, when the boys chased the girls on the playground."

"And ended up kissing them? Funny, I don't remember that happening in third grade."

"Okay, I got it that this is too soon for us to kiss. But what if we respectfully hugged each other?" I asked.

"We're talking one brief hug that doesn't turn into anything else, right?"

"Absolutely. That will be our official rule," I said softly.

"Okay."

I put my arms around her. "This does feel good!" I said.

"Yeah, it does. It feels, well, comfortable. Any other words come to mind?" she asked.

"It's like coming home after a long trip," I said. "But it does make me wonder what it would be like if we kissed. If you want, we could think of it as some kind of science experiment."

"A science experiment?" she asked with a big grin on her face.

I nodded. "I can talk with a German accent so it will seem even more scientific." I paused. "Ve vill now commence kissenze."

She couldn't stop laughing.

"Stoppen zee laufing!" I said. "I can't kissenze ven you laufing!"

That only made her laugh more.

But then we looked into each other's eyes. And that did it for both of us.

We were well on our way to our first kiss when Sara stepped out of the trees and yelled, "What are you two doing?"

"Nothing!" Mandy said, her face turning red as we moved quickly away from each other. "We were just, you know, resting up from our hike."

"Don't give me that! We've been standing here watching you both for a long time. How could you have anything to do with this jerk after what he said about Muffy?"

There was another girl from the ward with her. "Who's Muffy?" she asked. She was taller than either Mandy or Sara, had long blonde hair and was wearing a T-shirt that read, *Call me sometime.*

"Her dog that died," Mandy answered.

"Most everyone in the ward has already left," Sara complained. "I was worried about you two so we came looking for you. I thought you might have fallen or something. I didn't expect to see you making out with some guy you just met."

"We were not making out, okay?" I said. "We might have been talking about kissing one time but that didn't even happen."

"This is so unlike you," Sara said to Mandy.

We all started down the trail. "She's right. This is unlike me," Mandy said privately to me.

"Look, Sara, this could happen to anyone," I said. "Start running and I'll try to catch you. It'll be fun."

Sara glared at me. "And if you catch me, you think I'll let you kiss me?"

"No. I actually don't even want to kiss you."

"And you think I do?"

"No. You're still mad at me for making fun of your dog Muffy."

"Good job for saying Muffy," Mandy said to me.

"Thanks," I said.

I turned to the other girl. "Would you like me to chase you? Just to prove a point."

She got a big grin on her face. "You can chase me anytime, Big Guy! Oh, I'm Monica."

"Good to meet you, Monica. You ready to have me chase you?"

"I am!"

"Actually, I don't want you chasing Monica," Mandy said.

"Okay. I was just trying to make the point that playing tag is like a universal thing boys and girls do."

"You two are not little boys and girls," Sara said. "It's different now when a guy chases a girl. Especially if the girl is practically inviting the guy to make out with her."

"Give it a rest, okay?" Mandy grumbled.

When we got to the picnic area, I had to use the restroom. I could hear Mandy and Sara in a heated discussion.

"You think I'm not embarrassed?" Mandy said. "Well I am."

"How can you even stand him? What kind of a person makes fun of a person's dog that just died."

"He didn't know Muffy had died when he made fun of her name. And another thing, just because I let him hug me doesn't mean I like him that much. When I was a little girl, I let Santa hug me and I didn't even know him."

"What is wrong with you? I have totally lost all respect I ever had for you."

"It wasn't like all fun and games, okay? We had a serious talk too. His dad died when he was a kid, just like me with my mom."

"You don't actually like him, do you?"

Long pause. "I don't know. Maybe a little."

"Why? Give me one reason."

"Well, for one thing, he can keep up with me on the trail," Mandy said.

"Well, if he can do that, then by all means you two should definitely get married! I mean, c'mon, that's all that counts in life, right?" Sara said. And then she added, "How long does it take a guy to use a restroom anyway?"

I decided I'd better make myself known.

As we walked to the parking lot, I turned to Mandy. "Can we do something later on today?"

"Yeah, that'd be great."

"I'll follow you back to your apartment," I said.

"Yeah, sure. And then what?" she asked.

"What I'd really like to do is come back up here with you," I said.

"That sounds good to me."

"If you two come back here, I'm coming along as a chaperon," Sara said.

"Maybe we could do something on campus," I said. "I'm auditioning for an opera tomorrow, and I need to work on a couple of the songs. You want to help me with that?"

"Yeah, sure, as long as I don't have to sing."

"You won't."

"Okay. Follow me to our apartment and then I'll go with you," Mandy said.

"I'll ride with him so he'll have someone to talk to," Monica said with a big smile.

"You are not riding with him!" Sara called out. "You will ride with us where you'll be safe."

"I guess you'll be riding alone," Monica said. "Maybe some other time, though, okay?"

"Maybe so."

"Monica just graduated from high school," Sara said, saying it like that meant I shouldn't even talk to her.

"I actually graduated early. In January," Monica said.

"I could tell you were more mature," I said.

Monica smiled. "I am. I'm very mature for my age."

"Monica! Quit talking to that jerk! Get in! We're leaving!" Sara yelled.

I followed them to their apartment. When we pulled up and stopped, Sara quickly escorted Monica into their apartment, and Mandy came over to me in my car. "I need to change. But you probably shouldn't come in. If you do, Sara will make both of us miserable. That's what she does best."

"I'll stay here then."

While Mandy was gone, I sang to myself.

When she returned, it was like she'd changed identities. Very little was left of her Wyoming heritage. She was wearing a cream-colored shirt and tan slacks that would fit in anywhere on campus. Even so, she was still of course amazingly beautiful.

"You look good," I said.

"Thanks."

A few minutes later we entered the Harris Fine Arts Center. I usually practiced in one of the practice rooms, but as we passed the De Jong Concert Hall, I noticed it was open with the lights on. We went in. A custodian was replacing some aisle lights.

"Is it okay if I practice here?" I asked him. "I'll be trying out for an opera here tomorrow night, and I'd like to get used to the acoustics."

"Yeah, sure, go ahead. I'll be here for about an hour and then I'll have to boot you out."

"Thank you."

"I'll sit in the first row and be your audience," Mandy said.

"It'll be boring to you for a while because I need to warm up first."

"I'm good."

First I warmed up and then I worked on the song I'd sung to Mandy when we were on the cliff face. I had a recording of the piano accompaniment of "La Bohéme." It had been loaned to me by Dr. Evenson, the director of BYU's production.

When I finished, Mandy gave me a standing ovation.

There was one other song I needed to work on. It was a duet. "Come up here. I need you to sing something with me."

"Not so fast there, Cowboy! You promised me I wouldn't have to sing."

"Look, I went hiking with you and then I risked my life climbing some dumb cliff for you. The least you can do is sing with me for a few minutes."

"I'm no opera singer, okay?"

"It doesn't matter. Just do your best. Please. It'll be a big help to me if you do this."

She sighed and came up on stage.

"Oh, one other thing. The lyrics are in Italian," I said.

She fake slugged me. "Are you crazy? You're asking me to sing a song in Italian? The only Italian I words I know are pizza and spaghetti. You can't be serious! This is you trying to get even with me for making you climb that rock face, isn't it?"

"No, it isn't. Look, you can do this. It's like life, one step at a time. First, we'll just say the words together, one word at a time."

That took ten minutes.

"Good job," I said. "Now we'll practice your part of the song one measure at a time. Let's just say 'ah' instead of the actual lyrics, okay? So just sing what I sing."

We worked on that for twenty minutes.

"Now we'll just put the lyrics with the music, one measure at a time," I said. "I'll sing your part, and you sing it up an octave from me, one measure at a time."

It was hard for her but she didn't give up.

The next time she sang her part and I sang my part one measure at a time.

"I can't believe we're actually doing this!" she said. "This is starting to sound good."

"I know! You're doing great."

And then we practiced going all the way through it the way it would be sung on stage. We spent twenty minutes on that.

That was when the custodian told us he had to boot us out.

"Before we go, let us sing this for you."

"Okay." He sat down on the first row.

We made it through the whole thing without stopping.

"Sounds real good!" the custodian said.

"Can you let us be here for just another fifteen minutes and then come back and we'll sing it for you again."

"You know what? For you two I'll do that."

He left.

"Tell me what's happening here in terms of the story before we do this again," Mandy asked.

"Sure, no problem. Mimi and Rodolfo have fallen in love, but Mimi is sick so she's left him to live with a man who has lots of money and can afford to pay for her medical care. But when she gets worse, the man loses interest in her and throws her out. So she comes back to be with Rodolfo. They are together only for a short time before she dies. Okay, that's basically the story. The song we're going to sing comes in the first act. It's when they first fall in love. It's called "O soave fanciulla."

"What does that mean?" she asked.

"It means, 'Oh! lovely girl.' "Let's do it one more time the way it would be done in an actual performance. You stand there. I'll come behind you and stop just before I get to you, and start singing. You turn and come into my arms and we'll sing the duet facing toward the audience. And at the end we'll both embrace."

At first I was so focused on the technical aspects of what we were doing as we sang, but then near the end, it got to me. I'd gone my whole life being one of only a few guys in my school who took singing lessons. Before my mission I was the only one in my ward majoring in vocal performance. I worried that I'd never find a girl who appreciated what I loved, and who would be willing to marry me, especially since the only thing I wanted to do was to sing at the Metropolitan Opera House in New York City.

Why the Met? Because I'd grown up listening to the Metropolitan Opera radio broadcasts of operas on Saturdays, although it wasn't something I'd ever admitted to anyone in high school.

When the custodian returned, we did it again for him.

We finished the song in an embrace. This might have ended in a kiss were it not for the custodian giving us a standing ovation.

And so we bowed, thanked him for helping us and then left the concert hall.

I gave her a big hug. "You did so good!"

"Thanks! It ended up being fun. Can you teach me how to be a better singer?"

"Yeah, sure, let's go to one of the practice rooms downstairs."

In the practice room, I became her vocal coach. "Okay, you did great, but there are a couple of things we can work on that will make you even more awesome. The first has to do with your diaphragm."

"Okay, teach me."

"This is going to seem a little weird to you, but I need you to put your hand on my stomach while I sing a note. You okay with that?"

"I bet you say that to all the girls, right?" she teased.

"What other girls? I've been on a mission for two years. Look, I know this is a little awkward but I promise it will be both educational and appropriate."

She nodded. "Okay, show me exactly where you want me to put my hand."

I put my hand on my stomach. "Put your hand right here over my hand."

She put her hand in the same place. I then removed my hand and then sang a note.

"I can't believe it! You're all muscle here!"

"Yeah, pretty much. This is to show you that singers don't sing just with their mouths. They provide support with their diaphragms. I'll give you an exercise you can do to strengthen your diaphragm."

"Great, show me!"

"First, good posture. Okay, good. Now breathe in as deeply as you can and push your stomach out as far as possible. Like this."

"This isn't a good look for me, is it?" she joked.

"No, it's fine. Let's do it together. Deep breath, okay? Good. Now exhale slowly and pull your stomach in slowly…like this." I blew air out slowly.

We practiced this for a few more minutes. "You can do that anytime, like in class or when you're studying."

"This is great!" she exclaimed. "I am going to practice this every day."

"Good for you! Okay, now the next thing we need to talk about is posture. After that I'll also give you some singing exercises focusing on vowels. Vowels absolutely rule in singing. We spend as much time as we can on the vowels and as little time as we can on consonants. "

We spent ten more minutes on that and then, finally, we sang the duet again.

"Teach me another song," Mandy asked.

"Okay, this is from the fourth act. Mimi, on the verge of death has returned to be with Rodolfo. They sing a duet together and then she dies. The name of the song is 'Sono Andati?' I sang it to you this afternoon on the cliff."

"I'm not sure I can do this because of my mom."

"I understand. Let's work a little on it just so you can sense the great love they had for one another."

We went through the same process, one step at a time.

It took us nearly an hour to make it through one time.

I gave her a hug. "Thanks so much! You're such a fast learner. In another month or two, you could actually play the part of Mimi."

We started on our way out of the building. "Think about all we've both learned from each other today," she said. "This sure beats making out in a parked car for like hours at a time, right?"

I paused. "Uh, can I get back to you on that?"

She fake punched my shoulder. "What am I ever going to do with you?" she asked.

"Sorry. You're right though. We have learned from each other. That means we've both experienced growth. That is what should happen in a relationship."

"So now we have a relationship?" she asked sarcastically.

"I should have said friendship."

She nodded. "I'm okay with friendship."

We sang our first song two more times in the hall. I'd never been happier with a girl than I was with her.

As we left the building, she said, "Thank you for being my voice coach."

"It's only fair. You taught me to rock climb."

"True. We both learned and were taught by each other. How often does that happen?"

"Almost never," I said.

"I know."

"What do you want to do now?" I asked.

"I should probably go back to my apartment," she said.

I was disappointed. "Really?"

"I think so. We've been together for a long time."

"It's gone fast."

"Yeah it has." She sighed. "Actually, it's been amazing to be with you today."

"For me too," I said. "But, of course, there are other factors that will soon come into play. Like you're about to tell me that you're waiting for a missionary and that he gets home in a couple of weeks, right?"

"Not me. What about you?"

"No. Well if it's not that, it'll be something else," I said.

"So what you're saying is there's no way the two of us would ever get together," she said.

"Exactly."

"Based on what?" she asked.

"Based on the fact that this has been the best time I've ever had with a girl, so obviously the whole thing is doomed from the start," I said.

"I wonder what the deal breaker will be for us."

"I can't see anything now, but of course we've only just met."

After parking in her apartment complex's parking lot, we started walking toward her door.

"I think we should talk about if we're going to kiss at the door or not," she said.

"Okay."

"The main reason I'd recommend against it is because Sara will ask. And if we have kissed, she'll lecture me for hours, and I really need to get some sleep."

"I totally understand."

"Maybe if we could hold off for a few days or maybe even a week," she said.

"You know what? No problem."

"If you want though, you can give me a hug," she said.

"Thank you. That's very considerate of you."

We hugged for a while and then she said, "So, Cowboy, you want to go shoot some hoops?"

I started laughing. "How'd you know?"

She went inside and brought out a basketball. We went to the parking lot where there was a basket set up. We shot around for a while and then she breezed past me and went in for a lay-up, and made it.

"'Mandy 2, David 0," she said. "By the way, what do people call you?"

"David."

"I can't call you that. How about Davey or Davey Boy?"

"Between the two I'll take Davey."

She tossed me the ball. "I dare you to get past me, Davey."

"I don't want to get past you."

"You're supposed to get past me and go in for a lay-up."

"Why?"

"So we can be tied," she said.

I shot and quite by accident it went in.

"We're tied now," I said.

"Not for long, my friend, not for long."

She came fast at me, pivoted and went in for another basket.

"Mandy 4, Davey 2."

"Not bad."

"I know. I'm totally awesome!" she said.

"I'm your biggest fan," I said.

She kept dribbling as we talked. "No, my dad is. Sorry."

"Second biggest fan then."

"Actually that spot is open." She tossed me the ball. "Your turn."

I shot again and missed.

"Out of the day money, out of the average! All he gets is the hand you give him! Let's give that cowboy a great big hand! Yeah!"

"Where did that come from?" I asked.

"When we first moved to Cheyenne, I was on a rodeo team. That's what the announcer says when a bull rider falls before the time is up."

"I saw a movie about a cowboy once."

She started laughing. "Well there's nothing more I need to tell you, is there?"

"Nope. I even know what dogies are."

"What are they?"

"Small dogs."

She laughed, came up to me and messed up my hair.

We shot baskets for another half hour. At first I was a good sport about her being so much better than me, but when the score got to be 25 to 6, I was a little dejected.

"Okay, I give up. Can you show me what I can do to get better?" I asked.

"Okay, first of all, you need to follow through on every shot. Watch how I do it,"

We practiced that for a while.

She came up and patted me on the back. "Good job. One more thing you can work on is to be more relaxed. With you it's like you're saying, 'You stupid ball! Go in the basket this time or I will run over you with my car!'"

"It's not easy to look relaxed when you miss every shot," I said.

"Okay, watch how I do it."

We shot around some more.

"Good job. You're getting better," she said.

"Thanks. It feels better."

"Now it's your turn to teach me something, like how to dance."

"I'm sure you already know how to dance," I said.

"I mean like for on stage."

"I can show you something a girl in my class and I did for a high school talent show when we were both seniors."

"Great."

"So we're going to be doing hip hop. It's very simple. Step back, then the other leg joins, and then elbows up. I'll do it first: 5,6,7,8." I showed her the move.

We did that a few times. And then I showed her another part.

It took us about ten minutes before we could do the basic routine.

"Okay, this is for keeps. Five, six, seven, eight," I said.

"Sorry," she said once when she started on the wrong foot.

"It's okay. It's like repentance. We just start over again. 5,6,7,8."

It went better that time. "Okay, big finish here. Focus. That's it! Keep going! Yes, you did it! Good job!"

She gave me a high five. "Thanks for working with me! Can we do it again?"

"Yeah, of course. Absolutely. A little faster this time, okay?"

After ten more minutes, we had to stop to catch our breath. "You're amazing!" I said. "You learn so fast!"

"Thanks. This is so much fun! Can you show me more whenever we get together again?"

"Yeah, sure. We'll practice until we get good enough to do it for a ward talent show."

"I'm all for that."

"I can't believe what a fast learner you are," I said as I gave her a brief hug.

"I think it's more that you're a good teacher."

I looked at my watch. It was almost midnight. "I'd better get you inside your apartment before Sara freaks out."

"What do you think is happening here?" I asked as we walked back to her apartment. "I mean with us."

"I think we're having a great time together," she said. "The best time I've ever had with a guy."

"For me, it's like you're the girl I've always dreamed of meeting someday. Can I take you to lunch tomorrow? My treat."

"Sounds good. It's like I can't get enough of you."

"I know. That's the way it is for me."

She sighed. "Actually, there is something I should maybe tell you. Meeting you and having you keep up with me on the trail and everything else we did today was like an answer to a prayer I offered this morning."

"In what way?" I asked.

"This morning I was reading about Isaac and Rebecca. How the servant prayed and asked for a sign that the one Isaac should marry would be the girl who gave him a drink and watered his camels. Rebecca came and did exactly that, so the servant knew that she was the one for Isaac to marry."

"I knew I should have brought my camel today," I joked.

She shook her head. "This is serious. This morning I prayed that I could meet someone today that I could feel totally comfortable with." She sighed. "You know what? I think you might be my Rebecca."

"In what way?"

"I don't know how many guys I've left on the trail, panting for breath, begging for me to slow down." She paused. "And then you show up on the day I'd prayed for a sign."

"Interesting," I said.

She shook her head. "Sorry. I said too much, didn't I? You're freaking out now, right?"

"No, not really. Let me tell you about what I've always hoped for. My main goal in life is to be an opera singer. Tonight when we were singing together was the best time I've ever had with a girl. And right now I don't want it to ever end."

She paused. "So maybe we might someday, you know, actually get married?"

I took both her hands in mine. "It looks real good right now."

"I agree."

"This is so weird," she said.

"I know. It really is."

She sighed. "So if we're both thinking we might end up getting married someday, I wonder if that means we're engaged," she said.

I shrugged. "I have no idea. This is new territory for me. I suppose it could mean that."

"Well then, if we are engaged, maybe we should kiss at least once," she said.

I paused, trying to give the impression of being circumspect. "You know what? That does seem totally appropriate."

And so we kissed. It was a total game-changer for me. "So when's the soonest you think we could get married? How about like in a week or two?" I asked.

She started laughing. "Whoa there, Big Fella! This is like when I've been riding Dance-A- Lot all day. When we're not far from the barn, he starts galloping because he knows something very good is about to happen."

"I can't believe you're comparing me to your horse."

"That's a compliment actually. There are very few things I love more than Dance-A-Lot."

"Will he be coming to our wedding reception?" I asked.

She laughed "Yes, he will."

"Be sure and tell me which punch bowl he's drinking out of, okay?"

She laughed. "Why is it so much fun to be with you?" she asked.

"I'm wondering the same thing myself." I touched her face where her dimple was hiding.

"What are you doing?" she asked.

"I love your dimple. It's like a wonderful gift that is only shown to those who make you smile."

"Which you do quite often."

I touched her hair. "When we were hiking, when the sun was on your hair it would be glowing. It was spectacular!"

She shook her head. "This is a little weird."

"Let me just say I really like being with you."

She nodded. "Me too. A couple of times today I looked at you and thought, 'How did I ever get so lucky to be able to spend time with Prince Charming?'"

"Really? Not Winnie the Pooh?" I teased.

She shook her head. "You became my Prince Charming when you let me talk as long as I wanted about my mom. With everyone else, they'll give me like five minutes and then they say, 'How long has it been since she died? Maybe it's time for you to move on now.'"

"I would very much like being your Prince Charming," I said.

"That makes me happy. Can we go on a hike tomorrow?" she asked.

"Yes, of course. Especially if you'll let me chase you. And maybe we could practice singing too."

She nodded. "Of course. I know that's important to you."

"It is. Very important. This is what I've always dreamed of."

And so we parted.

When I got back to my apartment, my roommate asked how my time with Mandy had gone.

I shrugged. "It was okay I guess," I said with little enthusiasm. I decided it probably wouldn't be a good idea to tell him I was engaged to her. *I'll give it like a week before I tell him. No use rushing into anything.*

CHAPTER TWO

My first thought upon waking up the next morning was sheer panic. *I asked a girl to marry me after knowing her only a few hours? How is that possible? I don't even know her last name!*

At least I knew her first name was Mandy. I grabbed a ward list and went through it. I couldn't find any Mandy's but I did find two Amandas. I thought of sending a text message to each of them: "I didn't happen to propose to you last night, did I? Look, if I did, I'm real sorry. The doctor has me on medications and sometimes I do or say stupid, irrational things. So just forget about it if it was you. Nothing personal, okay? Have a nice day."

I went to the kitchen and poured some cereal in my bowl and then added milk. Instead of eating it though, I stared as the cereal slowly sunk to the bottom of the bowl. I could so relate with that.

There was a knock at the door. I opened the door, even though I was still in my pajamas. It was Mandy. Her hair was tangled like she'd just got out of bed. "You haven't told anyone about us getting engaged last night, have you?"

"No. What about you?"

She shook her head. "No. I woke up in the middle of the night and couldn't get back to sleep. I really think we should get to know each other a little better before we announce anything."

"I totally agree! So we're not engaged after all, right?"

"Oh, we can still be engaged," she said. "We just won't tell anyone about it for a while."

"Oh."

"You have New York Yankee pajamas?" she teased.

"Why yes, I do."

She started laughing. "I didn't think they made those in men's sizes."

"Well, as you can clearly see, they do."

"Will you be wearing your Yankee pajamas on our honeymoon?" she asked with a big grin.

I panicked. *You propose one time to a girl in a moment of weakness, and she never lets you forget it? What have I gotten myself into? And who does she think she is anyway, mocking my pajamas?*

And then it hit me. It wasn't just her having no respect for my pajamas. This is what married life will be like. Once I get married, my life will, for all purposes, be over. Well, not my entire life of course. Just the part that involves the freedom to do whatever I want to do whenever I want to do it. Like putting ketchup on scrambled eggs, which for some reason, women always hate. Or at least my mom does.

But that's not all. If I were married, I'd have to figure out how to pay for everything. My mom was paying all my college expenses but I doubted she'd do that after I was married, even though I'd need it more then.

And then there were the expenses of a honeymoon: renting a tux, restaurant, gas, wedding ring and hotel. And that's just the beginning.

And then there was life as a married student: rent, food, tuition for both of us, health insurance. And if she got pregnant, there would be no end to the expenses.

Before long I'll be driving a minivan with six screaming kids. And each kid will have an ice cream cone in their hand and they'll make everything a sticky mess on the interior which, of course, I'll have to clean up.

I had just turned 22 years old. With a little luck I could easily go to 30 before getting married. That means I could have eight years of blissfully going to college and then graduate school with my mom paying most of my expenses. And hopefully, sometime she'll even kick in enough for a better car.

Who is this girl and why is she talking about us being married? She's got some nerve. This is a total invasion of my privacy. Also, how can I find out her last name without making it obvious that I have no idea what it is?

I needed to get away from her. "I need to get ready for class."

"Yeah, me too. I just wanted to make sure you hadn't told anyone about us."

"No, I haven't. And I won't."

"Me either. I think it's for the best."

"I totally agree."

"Oh, It turns out I won't be able to eat lunch with you today after all, but can we still go on a hike later in the afternoon?" she asked.

I didn't see how I could say no to that. It would imply that I didn't want to ever spend any more time with her, which was mostly true. But if we did go on a hike, she might let me chase her through the woods again, and maybe even let me kiss her again, which of course I'd enjoy.

"Yeah, okay, I can work that in," I said

"Could you pick me up about two thirty?"

I nodded. "Yeah, sure."

I tried to hug her without actually touching any part of her body, which is always a little awkward.

While I got ready for school, I decided I'd officially end our engagement on our hike so I wouldn't have that hanging over me anymore.

A little before three o'clock we started on our hike at the same place where our ward had met the day before.

Mandy didn't run ahead of me this time. She stayed next to me. To be polite, I reached for her hand. She smiled as we held hands.

A short time later, she grabbed my hat and ran away. I thought about not chasing her, but I figured if I did that she'd suspect something was wrong. So I chased her and that made her start laughing again.

Unfortunately when I finally caught up with her, we ended up kissing. Also, when she smiled, her magic dimple appeared again. And the sun highlighted her hair like the day before. And we sang the opera arias we'd worked on the night before.

We climbed the rock face again and sat next to each other and planned our honeymoon. Don't judge me though. If a girl asks a guy where he'd like to spend their honeymoon, what's he supposed to do? It actually seemed very natural to talk about our honeymoon on that rock face. I'm not sure why.

On our way back down the trail, it didn't seem right to tell the girl I'd been kissing and planning our honeymoon with that I wanted to end our relationship. Besides, she was so happy, so bubbling with excitement, so full of life. For some reason she was even more beautiful on a hike. I have no explanation for that.

I'll break up with her...real soon, I thought.

There were many things I liked about what we'd done the two times we'd gone hiking. Chasing her through the woods, bellowing out like some villain how I was going to catch her. Also I liked that she was laughing as she ran away from me. I also liked it that she was okay with us kissing. And that she was so willing to let me teach her how to sing better. And also the help she gave me in shooting baskets the night before. Each of us had learned from the other. What if that could continue in a marriage?

"I have a question," I said as we drove back to campus.

"Okay?"

"How do you spell your last name?"

"Oh, you know, just the usual way."

I broke into a sweat. "The reason I asked is that there are...you know... several ways to spell that name. So I was just wondering which way you spell it."

She started laughing. "You don't actually know what my last name is, do you?"

I laughed. "Do you honestly think I'd be practically engaged to someone when I didn't even know her last name?"

She sighed. "The truth is, I don't know your last name either," she said.

"Oh, it's Lancaster. And yours is?"

"Wilson. Let me spell that for you. Whieillsohnned. The d and h are silent."

"Really?"

She started laughing and fake punched me on the shoulder . "No, it's just the regular spelling. Okay, we must promise that we won't ever tell anyone that we got engaged without knowing the other's last name."

"Yeah, it might cause people in our ward to mock us."

"Besides your name is there anything else I should know about you, in case anyone asks?" she asked.

"Well, one thing. I was a zone leader on my mission."

She started laughing. "You've wanted to tell me that since we first met, haven't you?"

"Not really. Oh, one other thing. I've never played a video game in my life."

"That's nothing to be ashamed of," she said.

"My mom always told me there were more important things to do than that," I said.

"Well, she was probably right."

"In high school that's all my friends talked about. And I just nodded like I knew what they were saying. I felt so out of it in high school."

"No problem," she said. "Here's one from me. In high school nobody ever asked me out. Not even once."

"How come?"

"I think mainly because everyone believed that I'd beat up a guy in school my sophomore year. What really happened is he tried to grope me in the hall on my way to class so I shoved him backwards. He fell and hit his head on the water fountain. They had to call an ambulance because of all the blood. He was out of school for a couple of days. When he returned, he had a big bandage on his head. He told everyone it was because I'd kicked him in the head when he was tying his shoe. She sighed. "After that, guys just seemed to avoid me."

"Their loss."

"Actually you're the first guy I ever kissed," she said.

I cleared my throat. "I see."

She stared at me, expecting a similar statement.

"I've kissed a few times but mostly to girls I hardly knew," I said.

She started laughing. "Oh, you mean like me, right?"

I was stumped how to answer that question, so I said, "Except now we know each other's last names. So that makes kissing much more appropriate."

"And, of course, the fact that we're engaged," she said.

I gulped. "Oh, yeah, that too." *Why does she keep bringing that up*? I thought.

When I dropped her off at her apartment, she told me she thought it would be a good idea for us to meet each other's parent before we announced our engagement.

I panicked. "You want to meet my mom?" I asked my voice cracking as I said it. "She lives in California. That's a long ways from here."

"Where in California?"

"San Francisco."

"That's not so far. Let's drive down there sometime. And, also, I want you to meet my dad, and you will. It's just that he's so busy now as attorney general. I'm thinking Thanksgiving might be a good time for us to get together with him. We could all get together at our place near Yellowstone National Park."

Thanksgiving seemed like an eternity away. I figured by that time we'd have already broken up. "Sounds good."

"I've got an idea," she said. "Maybe we could drive down to see your mom on General Conference weekend."

"The only trouble with that is that if I get a part in the opera we'll be practicing Saturdays."

"You won't be practicing the Saturday of conference, will you?"

"Maybe not," I muttered.

"Okay, we can leave Friday at noon, stay Saturday and part of Sunday, and then start back after lunch. We'll listen to the last session of conference in the car. We'll get back to Provo Sunday night."

The truth is I did not want my mom finding out about Mandy. I could imagine her asking me why "on earth" I would propose to a girl after only knowing her for only a few hours. I knew that telling her it was because I liked chasing her through the woods would not work with her.

"How does that sound?" Mandy asked.

"Well, my mom does a lot of traveling. I'm not sure she'll even be home that weekend."

"Why don't you call and ask her?"

"Yeah, sure." Although I said it, I couldn't imagine doing it.

She asked me when and where the tryouts for the opera were going to be held, so I told her.

I didn't even walk her to her door. I just dropped her off.

I had something to eat, changed clothes, and drove to the Harris Fine Arts Center. I warmed up until it was time for the tryouts to begin.

There were about forty people who had come to try out. Almost anyone who showed up would get a part in the chorus, but I wanted the lead part, that of Rodolfo. There were two other guys who were competitive with me, but I was fairly confident.

The first thing that happened for tryouts is that each of us sang something we had prepared for the occasion. Some were so bad that they'd only sing a few seconds before Dr. Evenson, the director, would call out, "Next!"

From their list of possible leads, Dr. Evenson and Dr. Freeman, his assistant, would have, for example, all the sopranos sing again, and then all the altos, all the baritones, and finally all the tenors.

An hour into the tryouts, I looked into the audience and noticed Mandy sitting a couple of rows behind the ones who were trying out.

She smiled and gave me a big thumbs-up.

What's she doing here? I thought. *Oh, I know. It's because she thinks we're engaged.*

After about an hour and a half, it came down to one other guy and me for the lead tenor part of Rodolfo. In terms of the lead soprano part of Mimi, there didn't seem to be a clear choice. One of the sopranos could sing but couldn't act. The other could act but sang off key some of the time. I figured that if either of them got the part, the audience would be cheering for Mimi to die, the sooner the better.

Dr. Evenson had each of the possible female leads sing a duet together with me, and then with the other guy.

It still wasn't working.

Finally out of desperation, he turned to those in the auditorium and asked "Have any of you ever sung this duet before?"

Mandy stood up. "I have," she said.

"Great. Get on stage and let me hear you and David."

I wasn't much worried she'd get the part of Mimi. I mean, c'mon, she wasn't even a music major.

Mandy and I sang "O soave fanciulla" a duet in Act One of *La Bohéme*. We'd practiced it the night before. It's where Rodolfo and Mimi fall in love after knowing each other just a few minutes. After being with Mandy for two days, I was less critical of that premise than I used to be.

At first Mandy was tentative and stiff but then I noticed tears in her eyes. We finished strong but by the end we were both emotionally drained. I held her in my arms. I was in love, either with the character she was playing, or with her.

There was silence in the theater. I could hear one of the girls crying.

Dr. Evenson was wiping his eyes. "What just happened here?" he asked.

Nobody answered.

"This, people, is the reason I got into opera!" he said. "For the emotion, for the honesty, for the truths that are revealed! I was very moved by what the two of you just did."

"Thank you so much," Mandy said.

"Yeah, thanks," I said.

"I do have some questions for you, though," he said to Mandy. "What voice training have you had that taught you how to project your voice so well?"

"Well, I got some in FFA."

"FFA?"

"Future Farmers of America. That was in Cheyenne, Wyoming my junior and senior year of high school."

"Did that involve singing?"

"No, it was a speech contest. The winners got to go to Washington, D.C. and give their speech to members of Congress, well at least to those from Wyoming."

"I see. Well, whatever they taught you was very good because your voice projects extremely well."

"Oh, and I did sing in choir in high school," she said.

"Good. Anything else?"

"Well, actually, I've started voice lessons here," she said.

I looked at her.

"From you," she said softly.

"You have the right equipment. It just needs to be honed a little," Dr. Evenson said. "You can have the part if you want it."

"Are you serious?" Mandy asked. She couldn't believe it either.

"Yes. You and David moved me so much tonight."

Dr. Freeman walked over to Dr. Evenson and asked quietly, "How can you think of giving the lead female role to someone who's never taken a single class in the Music Department?"

Dr. Evenson sighed. "You're right. It's just that I was so moved by what these two did."

"I understand, but doing this makes no sense and you know it," he said quietly.

Elizabeth, the soprano who could sing but couldn't act, stood up to confront Mandy. "I've never had you in any of my classes. What's your major?"

"Physical Education. I want to be a basketball coach someday," Mandy said.

"So you being in *La Bohéme* will not help you to teach the girls to dribble, right?" she asked sarcastically.

"Not really."

"How did you get interested in opera?" she asked.

"I pretty much have no interest in opera. My main interest is in David."

"And how long have you known him?"

"I met him yesterday at a ward picnic," Mandy said.

"So you came here tonight because of him and not because you actually wanted to be in the opera?"

"Yeah, that's right."

Elizabeth turned to Dr. Evenson. "I'm a senior vocal music major. Besides all the classes I've taken and all the choirs I've been in, I've been taking private lessons for the last three years. And you're thinking of giving this part to some wannabe basketball coach? Do you really think that's fair?"

He flinched.

"She's right," Mandy said. "Give the part to our spoiled little princess here."

"Excuse me! What did you call me?" Elizabeth belted out. She was small in stature but could project her voice to fill a theater.

"You heard what I said!" Mandy yelled back. "If you got a problem with that, Sista, then let's take this outside!"

Everyone, including me, was shocked. This was an opera tryout, not a promo for a wrestling grudge match.

"I've made my case. That's all I have to say," Elizabeth told Dr. Evenson.

"Give it to her," Mandy said to the director. "She wants it a whole lot more than I do."

"We really do need to talk," Dr. Freeman said to Dr. Evenson.

Dr. Evenson announced a fifteen minute break.

Everyone left the concert hall except for Mandy and me. Mandy went near the back of the concert hall and sat down. She had her head down and was working on taking long deep breaths like I'd taught her.

I sat down next to her. She had her head touching the back of the chair ahead of her. "You okay?" I asked.

"No."

Another few minutes went by. "Sorry," she said.

"What are you sorry for?" I asked.

"Everything."

"Could you be more specific?"

She sighed. "Calling that girl a spoiled little princess and offering to fight her outside might have been a little over the top."

I nodded. "Maybe so. At least here in the Music Department."

She stood up. "I need to apologize to her now."

"That might be a good idea."

We found Elizabeth in the hall with her friends.

"Go talk to her first for me. Okay?" Mandy said.

"Okay."

I approached Elizabeth. "Mandy and I both real feel bad about what she said to you. She'd like to apologize if that would be okay with you."

"Where'd you find this chick anyway? Passed out on some barroom floor in Wyoming?"

"No. We met at a ward opening social."

Elizabeth shook her head. "Sorry for saying that." She sighed. "Okay, I'll talk to her."

Mandy walked over to Elizabeth and her friends. "I am so sorry for losing my temper. I shouldn't have called you a spoiled little princess and I shouldn't have offered to fight you. Fighting is never the answer." She paused. "Well, not usually, that is."

Elizabeth nodded. "I accept your apology."

"Thank you very much." She paused. "You've got a great voice. I'm sure you'll be a huge success playing Mimi. I'll be sure to come and cheer you on. And, once again, I am so sorry for being such a jerk. My only excuse is that I was raised in Wyoming."

"Thank you for coming to apologize."

Mandy then sought out Dr. Evenson. "Please give the part to Elizabeth," she said.

"Would you be willing to be her cover in case she gets sick for one of the performances?"

"I don't even know what that means."

"Be her understudy just in case she gets sick some night."

"What would that entail?"

"Come to every practice. Learn her part so well you could do it at a moment's notice."

She looked at me when she said, "I guess I could do that."

"Good. Thank you."

And that's how it went. True to her word, Mandy attended every practice. She got free voice lessons from Dr. Evenson. She rehearsed with him during the time the rest of the cast had breaks.

Once or twice a week, she and I would ask the custodian to let us into the concert hall. We'd sing together. My feelings of appreciation for her grew during those times.

What we did together seemed to fuel our love for each other. Almost every Saturday we spent at least part of the day hiking. That helped assure her I was the man of her dreams. She attended every opera rehearsal and practiced with us. With the help of Dr. Evenson, her singing voice was becoming much better.

I had always hoped to marry a girl who could sing well enough that we could sing duets in church. I also needed a wife who appreciated opera enough to be willing to live in New York City with me. We weren't there yet but I had hopes.

I began each morning looking at selfies we'd taken when we were together. I did that right after my morning prayers. I'd sit on my bed and go through them all. Sometimes I'd kneel down and give thanks for having Mandy in my life.

Kissing became a regular part of our time together. She was more in the mood for that on a hike. Me after we'd sung together.

Of course we couldn't go hiking all the time. Sometimes it was raining or once, even snowing, but we always did something together. We'd sometimes go and shoot baskets. She told me I was getting better but the truth is I was never good enough to beat her. I was a good sport about it though, but it did begin to bug me. I regretted more than ever that my dad never helped me learn to play any kind of sports before he died.

I did practice every day shooting baskets though. Usually for a few minutes before I went to bed. And I was getting better at it too.

The opera took over our whole life but, even so, we still had other classes. We tried to study during our rehearsals but for the most part we couldn't get much done. And that meant that after we said good night to each other, we each had two or three more hours of homework before we could get any sleep. We were often getting by with just four or five hours of sleep a night.

One time on a Saturday after a short hike we went to the library to study, but Mandy kept falling asleep. I picked up her textbook to see what she was studying. It was a basic math textbook. I started working on the assignment and eventually finished it, and then returned to my own homework.

When she woke up, she looked down at the completed assignment. "Who did this?"

"The homework fairy. Cute little guy. He flew in, landed on the table, and did it all by himself."

She smiled at me. "I love the homework fairy!"

"I'll tell him if he ever comes by here again."

"This is the nicest thing anyone has ever done for me! Thank you."

"Don't thank me. Thank the homework fairy."

"Actually I'd like to hug the homework fairy and give him a big kiss."

"How about you kiss me and I'll tell him how amazing it was when I see him again?" I asked.

"Good idea."

I led her into the stacks of books until we were out of sight of anyone and then we kissed a few times.

"Libraries are so much fun!" I whispered in her ear.

She fake punched me and then said, "I'm so tired. Can we sit down on a couch and you hold me in your arms and let me fall asleep?"

I paused. "Yeah, sure. For how long?"

"A couple of days should do it. I'm so tired."

"I'll give you half an hour and then I'll wake you up. Before we leave here, I need to show you how to do problems like this. So you'll know, like for the test."

She fell asleep. It became a little uncomfortable holding her but I managed to get the job done.

A librarian saw us and came over. "The library is not a place for this kind of activity."

"I know but we're in the cast for *La Bohéme*. We're always either practicing or doing homework. Give us just a few more minutes and then we'll leave."

She nodded. "I love *La Bohéme*! Carry on," she said and then left.

A couple of days later while we were studying, I asked her, "What are you getting out of being in *La Bohéme*?"

"You mean, besides time with you?"

"Yeah."

"I'm making progress as a singer. This is the first time I've realized how much fun it can be to sing, to convey a message that is more powerful than just the words would be by themselves."

"I'm glad it's a good experience for you," I said. "I had hoped it would be."

"There's another aspect to it that applies to anything in life. Once you take something you're not good at and by hard work get better, then you're never the same because you know that no matter how difficult something is, whatever it is, you can go through the same process and succeed at that too. That I think is probably the most important thing I will take from this."

I smiled. "Like me with basketball, right?"

"Absolutely!" She gave me a high five.

One topic kept coming up in our discussions. Mandy kept asking me if I'd told my mom about her yet, and also about us wanting to come visit her over conference.

The last time she talked to me about it, she said, "Are you actually going to tell her about me, or am I just a diversion until the opera is over, when you'll break up with me and move on to someone else?"

"I promise I'll call my mom tonight," I said.

My mom usually goes to bed at nine thirty, so I called her at eleven o'clock her time, hoping I'd wake her up from a deep sleep and then I'd mumble something about Mandy and me, but she'd be too sleepy to ask me any questions or hopefully even remember I'd called.

"Is anything wrong?" my mom asked when she answered the phone. She sounded like I'd woken her up, which made me very happy.

"Oh, wow, it is late, isn't it? Sorry. I won't keep you long. I just wanted to tell you I've been seeing a girl. Her name is Mandy. We're both in the opera so we spend a lot of time together. She said she'd like to meet you sometime."

"Well, I am planning on coming to one of the performances, so I'll be able to meet her then."

"Great, Mom. Well, I don't want to keep you any longer, so goodbye!"

"Why does this Mandy want to meet me?"

I cleared my throat. "I guess maybe because, you know, we're starting to like each other."

"I'm sure that will fade after you're both done with the opera. Like with you and the girl who played Maria in *West Side Story* in high school. What was her name?"

"Francesca."

"Did you ever contact Francesca after *West Side Story* was over?" she asked.

"No."

"Exactly my point."

"You know what? You're absolutely right! Why didn't I think of that? That's such a relief! I'm so glad I called! Talk to you later, okay?"

"Is this Mandy majoring in music?" my mom asked.

"No, she's actually a physical education major. She wants to be a high school gym teacher and also coach a girls' basketball team."

"I assume then that you two are just friends, right?"

I sighed. "Yes. Mostly I would say."

"Is this getting more serious than just the two of you being friends?"

I knew this could drag on forever so because of Mandy introducing me to basketball, I went outside with my roommate's ball and began shooting free throws in the parking lot.

"Well, actually, it's sort of, well, you know, I would say, drifting a tiny bit toward the serious side."

Shot. Missed

"For just her or for both of you?" she asked.

Shot. Missed.

"Well, for both of us I would say. Of course it's way too early to tell."

"That happened when you were in *West Side Story* too. You told me you liked Francesca too, but of course nothing came from it. So I would say that as long as you're not engaged, I wouldn't worry about it."

"Of course! Why didn't I think of that? I'm so glad I called! Thanks so much, Mom. Well I won't keep you any longer! And again sorry for calling so late. Good night!"

"Wait! You're not engaged, are you?"

Shot. Missed.

Shot. Missed.

Shot. Missed.

"Are you engaged or not?" my mom asked again.

"I'm not exactly sure what you mean by that," I said.

"Are you and this future high school basketball coach engaged to be married?"

I cleared my throat. "Well, actually, that is, uh, you know, a little difficult to say."

Shot. Missed.

"Why would it be difficult?" she said. "You're either engaged or you're not."

Shot. Missed.

"Well, the thing is, she thinks we're engaged, but me not so much."

After a long pause, my mom exclaimed, "Oh my gosh! You haven't got this poor girl pregnant, have you?"

"No, Mom!" Out of frustration I threw the stupid ball at the stupid backboard as hard as I could.

"What's all that noise?" Mom asked.

"I'm outside in the parking lot, shooting baskets."

"Why are you doing that this time of night?"

Shot. Missed.

"Well, because Mandy is so much better than me at horse."

A long pause. "Is horse a term people your age use to describe out-of-control kissing, you know, like a runaway horse?" my mom asked.

"No, Mom! It's a basketball game."

"So why does this Mandy think you're engaged?"

Shot. Missed.

Shot. Missed

Shot. Missed

"Are you still there?" my mom asked.

"Well, the thing is, on the morning of the day we met she'd been reading in the Old Testament about, you know, that one guy who was trying to get a wife for what's his name."

"What are you talking about?"

I sighed. "You know, it's from the Old Testament. Somebody's servant was assigned to take some camels and go on a trip and find a wife for what's his name."

"It's hard to believe you graduated from seminary and served a mission. The man was a servant of Abraham, and he was sent to find a wife for Isaac. And the maiden's name was Rebekah."

"Yeah, right. Well, anyway this Rebekah came out and gave the servant some water and watered his camels and that was the sign the servant had prayed for."

"What has this got to do with this girl you just met?"

I took a deep breath. "Well, on the morning of the day we met, Mandy prayed to meet a guy she'd feel comfortable with. So we went on a hike and I was able to keep up with her, which nobody had ever done before. So she felt comfortable with me."

"Are you telling me that this Mandy thinks that, just because you could keep up with her on a hike, somehow that means you two are engaged? It sounds to me like this poor girl needs some serious and extensive counseling."

Shot. Missed.

Shot. Made it.

"Oh, yeah!" I yelled.

"What was that about?" my mom asked.

"I made one of my shots!"

I just hope the ball doesn't bounce back and hit you in the throat and make it so you'll never be able to speak or sing again," my mom said.

That brought back some painful memories. "I'm real careful, Mom! Just like I was when you only let me go to scout camp on the condition that I gargle with Listerine every morning and night! "

"It kept you healthy, didn't it?"

That set me off. I was practically yelling. "Do you have any idea how much grief I got from the other guys because of me gargling all the time?"

"That is certainly not something we need to talk about now. You could do so much better than this girl. By the way, Hillary is back from her semester abroad. She always asks about you."

Hillary was a girl I went to high school with. She accompanied me whenever I sang in church or in competition. Once when we were seventeen, we kissed a couple of times on her piano bench in the basement of her house. Unfortunately her younger brother caught us kissing once and told on us. After that her brother was assigned to be in the room whenever we practiced. If we even tried to sit next to each other at the piano, he'd yell to his mom that we were about to kiss, and she'd come down and tell us the practice was over.

"Say hello to her for me."

"Just because this poor confused girl, bless her heart, thinks you're engaged because you were able to keep up with her on a hike, that doesn't mean that you and she are actually engaged."

This conversation was not going the way I wanted. Out of frustration, I started throwing the ball at the backboard again and again.

Bang!

Bang!

Bang!

Bang!

A guy in a nearby apartment opened his window and yelled at me to keep the noise down. I thought of telling him off but didn't want to do that with my mom listening in.

"Mom, one thing though, I can't stand to be away from Mandy for more than a few hours. But with Hillary, I could be away from her for like months and not miss her."

"Maybe so, but this girl sounds extremely unstable. I'm sure they have trained counselors on campus. You must insist she meet with them on a regular basis until she gets over this delusion of hers."

That made me mad. "If you think she's unstable, well, I'm starting to wonder if I'm unstable as well." .

"Why would you think that?"

"Let me ask you a question. How would I be different if Dad hadn't died?"

She sighed. "I have no idea how to answer that question," she said.

"You think he might have let me go to scout camp without the stupid Listerine? Or that he would have taught me to play sports like all my friends' dads did? Or that he wouldn't have made me try out for all those operas?"

A long pause and then she said, "I did the best I could raising you. I'm sorry if that wasn't good enough."

That made me feel guilty. "I'm not blaming you, Mom. You were great. I just wish I'd had a dad who could give me his take on what a boy should be doing."

She started crying.

I knew this would drag on for hours if I let it. "Well, look, Mom, it's been great to talk to you but I need to get some sleep, you know, so I can do well in my classes, which I know is extremely important to you. Take care. Love you. Bye."

She called me back but I didn't pick up.

The next morning she did send me a text message. It read, "I'll ask Hillary to start shooting baskets now that I know how important that is to you as a criterion for choosing a wife." That was, of course, my mom being sarcastic.

The next day I told Mandy that I'd called my mom and told her about us.

"What did she say?" she asked.

"Oh, she asked how we met and things like that. She is very interested in meeting you when she comes to see *La Bohéme*."

A few days later, again on a hike, Mandy said, "I think it's probably okay now for us to get officially engaged."

I panicked. "Great, but actually, I haven't had a chance to buy a ring yet."

"I've got one here you can use. It was my mom's." She handed it to me.

I panicked. "This was your mom's wedding ring?"

"Yes, I've been saving it all these years just for this occasion."

This is getting way too serious! I thought. *She thinks we're actually going to get married. I need to quit fantasizing just about our honeymoon and face reality. Marriage is a big deal and it lasts a very long time and it often brings children and mortgages and vegetable gardens and home repair projects.*

"You should get down on one knee," she said.

I knelt down.

"Okay, go ahead," she said.

"I'm not exactly sure what to say."

"Well, basically, it's just 'Will you marry me?'"

I wiped the sweat from my forehead. After a long pause, I mumbled, "Will you, uh, I guess, you know, uh…?"

She stood up. "You're not sure you want to do this, are you?"

I stood up and started pacing back and forth. "Most of the time I'm for it. But sometimes I think about other things."

"What other things?" she asked.

"Like you getting pregnant and us not having any money. And what happens when your pickup breaks down, and we don't have any money to get it fixed?"

"We could use your car," she said.

"My car is a stupid piece of junk!"

"Actually, I worry too," she admitted. "Like what if it turns out after we're married that I find out I liked hiking with you more than I like being your wife and the mother of your kids?" she asked.

The phrase *the mother of your kids* totally freaked me out. Who says things like that anyway?

I sighed. "I like being with you but I'm not sure I'd like it if I always had to be with you," I said.

"I think it's okay to have misgivings. I told my dad about you and his response was, 'He wants to be an opera singer? There's nothing more worthless than an out-of-work opera singer. Does he have any marketable skills that he can use to support you and your kids?' So that got me thinking."

"I'll never be out of work."

"How can you say that? You're out of work now, aren't you?" she asked.

"No, but that's just because my mom is paying all my college expenses."

A long pause and then she shook her head and asked, "And that's okay with you?"

"Well, what about you? Isn't your dad paying for your expenses here?"

"Not really. The money I have is from what I earned working for him."

"Oh."

"What did your mom say about me?" she asked.

"Her first comment was, 'You could do a lot better than her.' But she always says that about every girl I start to like."

She glared at me. "And what did you tell her that would make her say that?"

"Nothing."

She shook her head. "You must have said something negative about me. What was it?"

"Nothing."

"Tell me what you said then."

"Well, I did tell her about you reading about Rebecca watering the servant's camels and how you prayed that something similar would happen to you, that you'd find a guy you felt comfortable with at the ward picnic, and how you did, and that was me because I could keep up with you on our hike."

She stood up and got in my face. "Are you telling me that your mom thinks that the only reason I want to marry you is because you can keep up with me on some stupid hike? She must think I need counseling, right?"

Unfortunately I waited a little too long before answering that question.

"She does, doesn't she? Don't lie to me!"

"Well, actually, she did mention that."

"You're afraid of your mom, aren't you?"

"Of course not. Why would I be afraid of her?"

"Because you know that if you ever stand up to her, she'll cut off all financial support and then you'll have to get a job like everyone else.

Let me make one thing perfectly clear! I do not want to marry a momma's boy! You got that?"

"I'm not a momma's boy!"

"Your mom pays your tuition, right?" she asked.

"Well, yeah."

"And the rent for your apartment?"

"Yes."

"And your groceries? And your car expenses? And your books?"

I cleared my throat and nodded.

"So explain to me again why you're not a momma's boy?"

"Because my dad had life insurance and my mom gets money every month from that. And so she transfers some of that money to me for my expenses here."

"Are the insurance checks written to you?" she asked.

"No, to my mom."

"That means it's her money then, doesn't it? Do you even have a part-time job on campus? Do you earn any money at all here?"

"No, but there's plenty of students here in the same boat."

Mandy thought about it and then said, "All right. One more question. Did you tell your mom that we were thinking about getting married?"

I didn't know how to answer that question. "Not exactly."

"And why is that?

I sighed. "Sometimes my mom is hard to deal with."

"Is it possible that you don't want to tell her about us because she's basically paying you to be a good little boy? If that's true, you are a momma's boy! And if that's the case, you can count me out of this whole deal!"

I stood up. "You don't know a thing about my family!"

"You're wrong! I know a great deal about your family now. Excuse me. I'm going for a run. I need to think through some things. Do not follow me!"

She was gone for twenty minutes. When she came back, she sat next to me. I thought about putting my arm around her but she was way too sweaty.

She sighed and then began. "Okay, first of all, I apologize for being such a witch about the relationship between you and your mom. My ideas about being self-sufficient might be warped because of being raised by my dad. But one thing is perfectly clear. I need to see you with your mom before I make any decision about us getting married. I also recommend you see me with my dad as well. So let's just stick with what we've got now and then we'll see what happens later."

I nodded. "Okay, we can do that."

A little before nine in the morning on the first Friday in October we began our trip to San Francisco to spend the weekend with my mom. We took Mandy's pickup because my car would never make it.

She drove the entire way. I kept offering to drive but she said she wasn't tired. That made me feel totally useless. Also, she had the annoying habit of going ten miles per hour faster than the speed limit. Secretly I hoped she'd get pulled over and be given a ticket but it didn't happen.

We didn't stop to eat because we wanted to save money for our honeymoon in case we actually did get married, which wasn't a certainty anymore. She'd brought a jar of peanut butter and some bread, and a knife, and plenty of water and some apples.

When she finished an apple, she threw the core out. I of course placed the core into a garbage bag. At first it made me mad about her littering, but then I thought about her growing up in Wyoming and decided that a random apple core off the side of the road in Wyoming might end up producing an apple tree and that would improve the entire state.

Just before we arrived, Mandy asked me to tell her something about my mom.

"She looks real good for her age. She spends a lot of time doing her hair and makeup."

"What color is her hair?"

"Blonde. It's always been blonde. It comes to a curl just at her chin. It always looks good."

"What else can you tell me about her?" Mandy asked.

"Well, she's in a book club. About ten women have been doing it for years. They meet once a month and discuss books that nobody else has any interest in. They often meet at our house. In high school I had to help her clean when they were coming. Maybe that's why I don't read much."

My mom lives in a historic San Francisco neighborhood with the houses very close to each other. By the time we arrived, it was almost nine o'clock at night their time.

"Mom, this is Mandy," I said at the door.

Mom was wearing a charcoal tweed pant suit. She gave Mandy a quick hug. "So good to meet you! I've heard so much about you. My name is Clareen. Please call me that instead of David's mom."

We sat down and talked for a few minutes. My mom asked when we'd left and how our trip had been. My guess is for her to make sure we hadn't left the day before and ended up staying the night in a motel.

My mom's cat Sylvester came in and made a nuisance of himself by walking on the back of the couch where we were sitting until finally Mandy picked it up and set it on the floor.

When the cat tried it again, Mandy asked if she should put the cat out.

"Oh no, Sylvester never goes out."

"We have cats at our ranch, but they never come in and we seldom even feed them. Sometimes they'll leave a dead mouse at our door though. I guess as a gift to us."

My mom scowled. "How interesting," my mom said. "But enough about cats, let's eat."

We sat around our small kitchen table. Even though Mandy and I were both starving, my mom fed us four small shrimp and a big helping of salad. For dessert she gave us each a fruit cup. It took Mandy about a minute to polish it all off. I was relieved she didn't wipe her mouth with her sleeve but used a napkin instead.

"Would you like anything else? I have more fruit cup," my mom said.

"I'm good," Mandy said. "Thank you so much."

A few minutes later, in the living room, while my mom had left us to get scrapbooks of me in operas and other music events, Mandy leaned over and whispered, "I'm so hungry! I need meat and potatoes! You've got to get me out of here so I can eat!"

"Okay, we'll go in a few minutes."

My mom returned and spent the next hour explaining in great detail each picture of me playing the part of a child in an opera scene.

"Oh, look, there you are again!" Mandy said after my mom showed her one of the many photos. "Oh, and this time you're in a dress! Oh, that is so cute!" she said sarcastically.

"It wasn't a dress," I said. "It was a kilt. This was an opera about Scotland."

"He was a young prince," my mom said. "He was killed in the first act."

"That must have been such a relief to get knocked off so soon!" Mandy said.

An awkward silence followed. "Why would you say that?" my mom asked.

"Well, it meant he wouldn't have to go on stage again wearing a dress. Oh, by the way, nice legs, Bro!"

"You don't seem to have much interest in opera," my mom said.

"Well, actually, I'm in an opera with Davey Boy. And he and I will be performing together if the lead soprano gets sick, which I'm working on. I try to get as many sick people in the cast and crew around her as I can so they can cough on her."

"I certainly hope that isn't true," my Mom said.

"No. In Wyoming we call that cowboy humor."

My mom sighed. "In California we call it cruel and insensitive."

Page after page, explanation after explanation, Mom went through my short career as a child singer. And then she shut the book. "And then his voice started to change and all this was suddenly over."

Mandy laughed and fake slugged my shoulder. "Puberty, hey, Bro? I'm so glad you went through it. It will make our honeymoon a lot more fun, if you know what I mean!" She then punched me on the shoulder and laughed.

My face, as well as that of my mom's, turned red.

My mom had had enough. "Well, it's late. I need to get to bed. Maybe we should have family prayer now. If it's okay, I'll offer it."

My mom's prayer was basically to bless us all with a clear mind so we won't make some stupid mistake we'll regret for the rest of our lives.

After the prayer, my mom hugged me, briefly touched Mandy's arm and said, "I am assuming I can trust you both to honor your baptismal, and in the case of David, your temple covenants tonight."

And with that my mom left.

"Let's get out of here! I'm starving!" Mandy said as she ran for the door.

I followed. "Is it okay if I drive? I know my way around here."

"No, I'll drive, but you can give me directions." Once we were on the way, she unloaded on me. "No son of mine is ever going on stage to sing some stupid song wearing a dress!"

"It was a kilt. That's what men and boys wear in Scotland."

"I don't care what it's called. If it looks like a dress, it's a dress!"

I shrugged. "Whatever."

"And what was your mom's prayer all about? She was praying that we'll keep our hands off each other, right, so I won't get pregnant, because then you'd have to marry me, right?"

I sighed. "Maybe so."

I took her to a Five Guys restaurant. She ordered two large burgers and an order of fries. "What do you want?" she asked.

I figured she'd be mad if I ordered a shrimp salad. "I'll take a burger and fries."

Our food came fast. She hurried to a booth, sat down, folded her arms for like two seconds, and then took a huge bite of one of her burgers. "Oh my gosh! This is so good!"

By the time she started on her second burger, she'd slowed down. "Sorry."

"No problem."

"Let me be perfectly honest," she said. "Being with your mom has been a little stressful for me."

"Yeah, I know. It's stressful for me too."

"It's not that she's a bad person. I know she loves you. It's just that growing up you didn't have a dad around to balance things out."

"True."

"And I didn't have a mom around to balance my dad's influence." She sighed. "So now we're both freaks of nature."

"Maybe together though we'll be able to make it...for us... and our kids," I said.

"Maybe so," she said, wiping her mouth with her sleeve. It was okay, though. She was raised by her dad. She slept in a barn with horses and in the summer camped in the woods for weeks at a time. But even with all that, she was still spectacularly beautiful.

"Come sit next to me and I'll show you how I start my day," I said.

I went through all the selfies I'd taken of her and me together.

And then I asked, "What's it like to be you? You're so amazing! Every morning when I look at these I see your beauty, remember your faithfulness in keeping the commandments, and how much fun we have together, how we make each other laugh, and how we both teach and learn from each other. That is so rare. I am so grateful for Heavenly Father allowing me to be with you. To just say I love you does not do justice to the way I feel about you. I love you so much."

She rested her hand on my arm. "I love you too. You were an answer to prayer for me. You know what? I wish we could just get married, like today."

I nodded. "I actually think a lot about us getting married," I said.

She got a silly grin on her face. "Tell me, Davey Boy, what part of our wedding day do you think about the most?"

I was not going to go there. "How beautiful you'll look in your wedding dress. Also I try to imagine all the beautiful flower arrangements and decorations at our reception."

She fake punched me on the shoulder. "You expect me to believe that all you think about is my dress and all the flowers and decorations? Give me a break."

"Hey, c'mon, flowers are my life."

"Yeah, right!" she said sarcastically. "Look, you don't fool me! You're thinking most about our first night together, right?"

I nodded. "I try to imagine all the flowers that will be in our room on our first night together." I sighed. "I just hope there's dahlias."

She leaned close to me and breathed into my ear. "Still thinking about flowers, Cowboy?" she asked seductively.

I cleared my throat. "Not so much now," I said.

She moved away from me. "Good! You want the rest of my second burger?"

"No, but thanks anyway."

We rode back home, shared a goodnight kiss in her pickup and then entered the house.

I walked her to her room and said goodnight, then went to my room, and got ready for bed.

She was staying in what had once been my dad's office on the first floor. She'd be sleeping on a couch that made into a bed. Usually on one wall were photos of my dad and also some of his awards. For Mandy's visit, however, my mom had removed them all and, maybe because Mandy was from Wyoming, had replaced them with paintings and photos of mountains that had been in his office when he was still alive. Mountains I'd never climbed, rivers I'd never forded and trails I'd never hiked.

Lately I'd begun to wonder how I'd have turned out if my dad hadn't died. Would I have chosen vocal performance as my major, and if not, what major would I have picked? He'd majored in business. Maybe I would have picked that too.

I also worried about what my mom's evaluation of Mandy would be. I didn't think she'd tell me while Mandy was with us, but it would come, probably over the phone. Basically it would be that although Mandy has many good qualities, I could do much better than her by marrying Hillary. And then she'd sigh and say what she always said, "That's all I want for you...just to be happy."

I knelt down and prayed that this visit wouldn't mess things up between Mandy and me.

And then finally I fell asleep.

At seven the next morning, there was a knock on my door.

"Come in," I said.

She opened the door but didn't come in. "I'm not sure your mom would approve of me being in here."

I tossed a pillow at her. She closed the door behind her, picked up the pillow and threw it back at me. A minute later we were having a full-blown pillow fight. We each kept shushing each other so we wouldn't wake my mom.

"You want to go running with me?" she asked.

"Yeah, sure. Give me a minute."

"I'll be outside on the steps," she said, and then left.

My minute lasted a little longer since I didn't have anything in my closet that joggers would wear. I finally picked out a pair of dress pants and a long sleeved white shirt along with my regular shoes. But to my credit I rolled up the sleeves.

"Are we going formal today?" she asked when I stepped outside. "The reason I ask is because I didn't bring a church dress."

"It is what it is. Let's go."

"I'll go slow for you so you can point out interesting historical sites we pass along the way," she said.

And so we ran...and ran...and ran. It didn't matter to her if we were going uphill or downhill because she kept the same speed all the time.

After fifteen minutes, she stopped to let me catch up.

"Please, can we just walk for a while?" I pleaded, trying to catch my breath.

"Yeah, sure. So this is San Francisco, right?"

"I guess so, unless we've passed city or state boundaries."

She laughed. "Do you know what I appreciate about you? That you try very hard to keep up with me. I've never had that experience with a guy before."

"It's because I love you."

"I know. And it's why I'm in the opera as a backup. I'm doing that for you."

"I know."

"When's the soonest we can leave to go back to Utah?" she asked.

"Well, tomorrow after the morning session. How would that be for you?"

"Actually I'm thinking it should be sooner than that," she said.

"How soon?"

"Now?" she said. "Sorry, just kidding."

"Why don't you like my mom?" I asked.

"I think it's mainly because she doesn't like me."

"How can you say that?" I asked.

"Her prayer last night. Let me paraphrase it for you. 'Bless my clueless son so he won't marry this dreadful girl and regret it for the rest of his life.'"

"Maybe so."

"What was a reasonable request you asked her growing up that she said no to?" she asked.

"When I turned twelve, I wanted to go to Boy Scout camp," I said.

"What were her reasons for turning you down?"

"She said the woods were full of germs and I'd probably get sick and die."

"So you didn't go?" she asked.

"Not when I was twelve."

"I feel so sorry for you."

"She did let me go when I was fourteen, but she made me promise to gargle with Listerine every morning and night. You can imagine what the other guys in the troop said about me doing that all the time."

Mandy shook her head. "I'm sorry she did that to you. Can you see that always following your mom's advice might be disastrous in your life?"

"Yeah, I can see that." I sighed. "How about we leave to go back to Utah right after the morning session today?"

"Great idea! And to show you how much I'm willing to reach out to her, whatever she serves us for lunch, I'm going to eat."

"That's very kind of you."

"I try to do my part," she said.

"Thank you. I love you."

"I love you too." She stood up and stretched her leg muscles for a couple of minutes.

"Okay, let's run again," I said. "This time I'll take the lead. This time try and keep up, okay?"

She started laughing.

Because I was ahead of her, we went much slower, but every few minutes, she'd call out to me, "Slow down! You're going too fast. I can't keep up with you."

And then we'd both laugh. And I was in love all over again

We stopped along the way and did some selfies of us, which I added to my collection for my morning Mandy ritual.

When we made it back home, my mom was waiting for us. "I was so worried you'd been in some kind of an accident. I was about to call the police and ask them to look for your bodies along the side of the road."

"We were fine, Mom," I said.

"You were gone so long. You didn't stop some place along the way, did you?"

"Why would we stop, Mom?" I asked.

My mom shook her head. "I have no idea what your generation does these days."

"Oh you mean like if we'd stopped at a motel?" Mandy asked.

My mom nodded. "Or some other place where you could be alone together."

"We didn't actually do that but, hey, thanks for the suggestion. Maybe we'll do that on our way home," Mandy teased.

My mom sighed and shook her head.

"She was just kidding, Mom," I said.

"I certainly hope so. Also, I noticed a pillow on the floor of your room this morning. What was that all about?"

"We had a pillow fight," I said.

"You were in my son's room?" she asked Mandy.

"Just long enough to have a pillow fight, and then to ask him if he wanted to go running with me."

"I didn't think I would have to tell you to stay out of my son's room," my mom said.

"Sorry."

"I threw the first pillow," I said.

"They still teach students at BYU about the Honor Code, don't they?"

"Mom, just let it go, okay?" I said.

My mom sighed. "I can see that I'll just have to stay up later tonight and get up earlier tomorrow morning."

Mandy glared at me. I didn't say anything so she did. "Actually you won't need to do that because we're leaving this afternoon," Mandy said.

My mom shook her head. "I'm sure that can't be true. David needs to go to the priesthood session tonight. I'm sure that's not important to you but it is to David because he honors the covenants he's made in the temple."

They both looked at me to see what my reaction would be. Would I please my mom or my future wife?

Before I did either, Hillary, a friend from high school, came in from the kitchen, carrying a tray of food. "Surprise!" she called out.

"Guess who dropped in unexpectedly while you were gone," my mom said. Of course I knew she'd called Hillary to come and rescue me.

"Hello, David."

"Hello, Hillary."

Hillary was almost as tall as me, had long hair which was mostly brown but had streaks of blonde. She was wearing a long sleeve loose-fitting purple shirt that made her look like royalty. She was also much better looking than she'd been in high school. I thought of telling her that but knew that wouldn't make Mandy happy.

"This is my friend Mandy," I said to Hillary.

"Oh, yes, I've heard so much about you," Hillary said.

I glared at my mom. "Yes, I'm sure you have."

"Hillary knows how much I like sushi," my mom said. "She made up some for her family and has just brought some over for us to enjoy." She turned to Mandy. "Do you like raw fish?"

"Don't know. I've never had it. Because of all the terrible diseases that you can get even from the fish we catch in Wyoming, we always cook our fish."

"Oh, you must try it. David has always loved sushi, haven't you, David?"

I shrugged. "It's okay I guess."

Hillary came over to me. I stood up and she gave me a big hug. "So good to see you again!"

"Yeah, you too, Hillary."

"Your mom has told me you're playing the lead role in *La Bohéme*," Hillary said. "How wonderful! I must say I'm not surprised."

"Thanks."

"David, why don't you sing what you sang at high school commencement and have Hillary play the accompaniment," my mom suggested. "I've kept the music here in the piano bench all these years. I take it out sometimes just to cherish once again that sweet memory of the two of you making beautiful music together."

Mandy flashed a cynical smile. "So you two made beautiful music together? I'd sure like to know more details about that!" Mandy said sarcastically.

"It means exactly what it says," my mom muttered.

While I was singing with Hillary accompanying me on the piano, Mandy broke up some of the sushi into small bits and put it into a paper napkin, formed it into a ball, tied it to a string she got from the kitchen and then started to drag it around on the floor as our cat tried to capture it.

When we finished, my mom stood up. "Encore! Encore!"

"Yeah, it was real good," Mandy said in a monotone voice.

"When Hillary accompanied you during commencement, it was such a precious moment for me," my mom said.

The cat lunged at the ball of sushi, split the napkin apart, and started to eat it.

"Is that some of Hillary's sushi she brought over for us?" my mom asked.

Mandy laughed. "Yeah, it is. Your cat is having a great time with it too!"

"I was hoping to have that later for a snack," my mom said.

"Well you're going to have to be faster than the cat then!" Mandy joked.

That made me laugh. My mom scowled at me, sighed, and shook her head.

"I'd better go," Hillary said. She turned to Mandy. "Great to meet you!"

"You too," she said, still teasing the cat.

"David, why don't you walk Hillary to the door?" my mom said.

I nodded, walked her to the door, gave her a quick hug, and said goodbye.

"Call me sometime," she whispered in my ear. "That is, when you're not engaged. Oh, my brother Billy is on a mission so he won't bother us anymore when we're downstairs, you know, at the piano."

"Oh," I said, starting to blush.

She whispered in my ear. "Also, I want you to know that I'm practicing shooting free throws, like your mom suggested. I know that's important to you although I'm not sure why."

"I'll keep that in mind."

When I returned, my mom said, "Tell me about this pillow fight you two had this morning."

"Davey Boy threw the pillow at me and then I threw it at him. That happened several times. That was about it."

"Was my son in his pajamas when you entered his bedroom?" my mom asked.

"Yes, he was in his New York Yankees pjs. Oh, I have a question about those pajamas. I assume that when you bought them, they were footie pajamas but then when he'd grown out of them, you cut off the feet part. Is that right? How old was he when you did that? My guess is just before he left on his mission, right?"

"They were not footie pajamas!" I complained.

My mom shook her head. "The issue here is that you were having a pillow fight in a bedroom with my son in his pajamas and you two not even married," my mom said. "There are some things that should only be done with those who are married."

"Are you saying that we need to meet with our bishop and confess we had a pillow fight?" Mandy asked sarcastically.

"Not if that was all that happened."

"That's all that happened, Mom," I said.

"Then I will accept that explanation. But enough of that. Right now we need to change attire."

"You got a flat tire? Let Davey and me change it for you," Mandy said.

"I meant the word attire which means clothing. David and I feel it shows more respect for our leaders if we're dressed in our Sunday best when we watch conference."

Mandy's mouth dropped open. "You do realize they can't see us through the TV, right?"

"It's just something we've always done," my mom said.

Mandy shook her head. "You two can do whatever you want but I will be staying in my present attire."

"I see. I suppose you'll also be munching on snacks during conference as well, is that right?" my mom asked.

"Yeah, probably so, if I can find anything good to eat. You don't mind if I look, do you?"

My mom sighed. "You do whatever you want, but David and I will be fasting."

The truth is my mom and I had never fasted during general conference. "I'm not going to fast, Mom."

"I see." She gave a prolonged sigh and then stood up. "Perhaps then I will watch conference in my room so I can more fully have the Spirit in my life."

Mandy got a huge grin on her face. "Great idea! Oh, be sure to wave and say hello to all the brethren for us, okay?"

Mandy and I watched conference in the living room without saying much. After a while, she came and sat next to me and I put my arm around her. I tried to kiss her during a rest hymn but she wasn't in the mood. We both fell asleep during the second hour but when we woke up, we promised each other we'd get the talks online and read them.

After the morning session, we thought my mom would come out but she didn't so we scrambled some eggs and made toast. Mandy couldn't believe we didn't have bacon.

We were about to sit down and eat when my mom came out. "Actually, I've planned a meal for us for lunch."

"Really? Short fast, huh?" Mandy asked.

My mom glared at her.

"We don't have to eat this," I said, referring to the food we'd fixed.

"It will just take a little while for me to fix what I had in mind."

"Can we help you?" Mandy asked.

My mom sighed. "No, I can do it. Perhaps David could show you our garden in the back."

We spent all of ten seconds in the backyard before Mandy told me she needed to take a walk.

Her walk made me run to keep up.

After a few minutes, I said, "We should have stayed to help my mom in the kitchen."

She stopped, turned to me, and glared. "After all these years with her, you still don't get it, do you?"

"Get what?"

"Whatever you do, it will be the wrong thing. Her goal is to make you feel guilty all the time so you'll continue to do things her way."

"And how is that different from what you're trying to do with me now?" I asked.

She threw up her hands. "That's it, Cowboy! I've had it! I'm so out of here! Why don't you go ask Mommy Dear to buy you a plane ticket back to Utah? See you on campus sometime! Oh, and if I still can, I'm bailing from the opera too!"

Mandy hurried inside and got her stuff and left without saying anything more to me.

I couldn't believe she'd left me.

I went in our backyard and started to pick weeds from my mom's flower garden. That was one of my chores in high school, and although my mom hadn't asked me to do it, I thought I should do it for her.

But somewhere in the process, I started ripping out both the weeds and the flowers. Within a couple of seconds though, I felt awful for what I was doing to my mom's flower garden so I stopped, then tried to replant the flowers I'd pulled out, but some of the stems were bent so much that I had to use rocks to prop them up so they wouldn't flop back down. And some I had to throw away.

Mandy thinks my mom wants me to feel guilty? Well, actually, I do feel guilty now! I feel guilty for attacking my mom's flowers! I feel guilty for making Mandy mad at me! I feel guilty because I don't want to lose my mom's financial support! And now Mandy is on her way back to Utah. So I'll have to ask Mom for money to fly back. Then she'll tell me I should have discussed with her who to marry. Which of course is Hillary. I also feel guilty for even thinking of going over to Hillary's house now and asking if we could go in her basement and practice, just to see if we'd end up making out again like we did that one time in high school. What is wrong with me? Am I really that shallow?

I managed to get my mom's flower garden to look almost the way it had been, except for a few rocks propping up some of the flowers.

A few minutes later, my mom came outside. I stood in front of her flowers so she wouldn't notice the damage I'd done.

"Where's Mandy?"

"She left to go back to Utah."

"Why?"

"We got into an argument."

"Do you want me to call Hillary and ask her to come over and comfort you?"

"No, Mom! I want you to stay out of my life!"

"Does that mean in terms of paying your tuition each semester and giving you money for your monthly expenses?"

What other choice did I have? "Yes."

"All right, if that's what you want, I'll be quite happy to do that."

She went inside.

Oh, that's just great! Now I'll have to get a job. I won't have any money to fix my stupid car so I'll end up junking it. So I'll be left with no car, no spending money, no private voice lessons, no pizza deliveries late at night, no more down-loading operas, no more subscription to Opera News, and no girl to spend time with. My stupid life is essentially over!

The only positive thing I could think of this is that maybe Mandy would be glad to find out I wasn't a Momma's boy anymore.

So I called her.

"What do you want?" she practically yelled.

"Can you come back and pick me up and take me back to Utah with you?"

"Isn't Mommy Dear going to buy you a plane ticket?"

"No. I asked her to stay out of my personal life. She asked me if that meant not helping financially with my education from now on, and I said yes. So, bottom line, I'm on my own now."

"I wouldn't worry about that, Bro. Just do whatever Mommy says from now on and she'll change her mind and keep the money coming. Of course I'll be out of the picture but you can always go back to Hillary and make beautiful music together again like you did in high school."

"I don't care about Hillary! I love you and I want to marry you!"

"Mommy's not happy about that, is she? That's why she threatened to cut off your money. So it's either her money or me. So what's it going to be?"

"I can't live without you."

Mandy paused. "Are you sure about that?"

"I am. It's time for me to grow up."

"Sounds like a good idea for both of us."

"Maybe so."

"Okay, look, I'm at Five Guys," she said. "Give me a few minutes and I'll pick you up. You want me to get you a burger, fries, and a drink?"

"Yeah, that'd be great."

"Okay."

"Also, I think we need to decide if we still want to be engaged," she said.

"Why?"

"Because with your mom being against us getting married and also her threatening to stop supporting you financially, in a week or two you might not be sure if you want to continue our relationship because you always do what Mommy wants, right?"

"Not anymore."

"I hope that's true, Bro. So, anyway, I'll see you soon," she said.

I went in and packed, knocked on my mom's door but she didn't answer.

"Mom, I'm leaving soon. Mandy will be taking me back to BYU. It'd be good if we could talk before I leave."

My mom opened her door. "I can't. KSL is doing a special about the Tabernacle Choir's recent trip. You should come and watch it with me."

"No, I got to go now, Mom. See you. Love you."

"Love you too."

I grabbed my bag and went outside and sat on the steps waiting for Mandy to show up.

When she pulled in front of the house, I got in. "Let's get out of here."

We didn't talk much as we started on our way back to Provo.

Ten minutes later though, Mandy turned to me and said, "We've got to go back."

"How come?"

She sighed. "I will not be the one who comes between you and your mom. Not now. Not ever."

"But she was the one at fault."

"It doesn't matter. You're all she has. If she loses you, she will have lost everything that gives meaning to her life."

Mandy drove back to my mom's place.

When my mom opened the front door, Mandy said, "May we come in? We've come to apologize."

"Please come in."

My mom invited us to sit down. "May I get you anything?"

"No, we're fine. Let me just begin. It still looks like David and I still might get married, although that could certainly change. It's on and off with us, depending on the day."

My mom nodded. "I understand."

"If we do get married though, I don't want to come between you and your son. I think we should both work hard to see that doesn't happen. I see so many good things in David, and I'm sure you're responsible for most of those things. I don't want us to be enemies. I also don't want you to feel that you'll never be welcome in our home. You will always be welcome."

"Thank you."

"Does it really matter that I prefer meat and potatoes, and you like salads? I mean, who cares, right?"

"That's right. It doesn't matter. What matters is that we respect each other."

My mom got up to hug Mandy but Mandy stepped back so she was behind me. So my mom hugged me. Mandy momentarily did rest her hand on my mom's shoulder though. "You're the mom, and I'm just a friend of your son. A very good friend as it turns out. But even so, I think we need to let David figure out what's best for him."

"I agree."

"Well, Davey Boy, do you have anything to say?" Mandy asked.

I cleared my throat. "Well, uh…I'm just glad that you two are getting along better now."

"That's it? That's all you've got to say?" Mandy asked. "Okay then, let me ask you a question. Are you going to let your mom or me decide your future?" Mandy asked. "Because, either way, when I see that in a man, I call it weakness."

I took a deep breath. "Okay, Mom, how about this? If you can cover my tuition for winter semester and my living expenses for January, I'll take over from there. How would that be for you?"

"If that's what you think is best, I can do that," my mom said.

"I like that decision on your part, Bro," Mandy said.

Mandy and my mom rescued the breakfast that we'd cooked earlier and put in the refrigerator. So we ate that, hugged, and said our goodbyes.

And then we left. On our way out to her pickup, Mandy told me she was tired and asked if I'd drive while she took a nap.

"Thanks, I would like to drive your, you know, rig."

She laughed. "You've never in your life ever said the word rig before, have you?"

"No, but I've seen plenty of people say it in commercials."

She smiled and shook her head. She gave me the keys and we got in. I drove. After a few minutes she fell asleep.

CHAPTER THREE

I drove for three hours and then Mandy woke up and offered to drive. So I pulled over and we switched.

"What were you thinking about while I was sleeping?" she asked.

"How impressed I am that you realized we needed to go back and apologize to my mom. I never would have thought of doing that."

"Why's that?"

"Because I thought we were in the right and my mom was wrong, so an apology wasn't necessary."

"You don't apologize only when you're wrong."

After a long pause, I said, "Oh."

"It might be good for you to learn that lesson now, before we're married."

"Do you ever worry about us being married?" I asked.

"I did, but now not as much. I knew I didn't want a momma's boy for a husband but that is what I was starting to see in you. But today when you told your mom your plan for you to become self-sufficient, I've got to admit, I was impressed. If you actually meant what you said."

"I did mean it."

"Don't get me wrong. You should respect your mom. You should ask her for advice at times. But after we're married, we shouldn't depend on her emotionally or financially." She paused. "I think the expression is 'Man up.'"

I smiled. "And what makes you so qualified to lecture me about being a man?"

"Well, I was raised by my dad. He's very independent and I admire him a great deal."

"Okay."

"One word of caution though. Don't replace one momma figure, your mom, for another momma figure, me. Okay?"

"This gets tricky, doesn't it?" I asked.

"Yeah, afraid so."

I sighed. "This is way more complicated than I ever thought it would be. But we'll work things out. One thing I especially like about you is I've always wanted to find a girl who loved opera and could sing."

"News flash—I love you. Opera not so much."

"With me it's I love you. Not so much running up mountains."

She laughed. "So we really have a lot in common."

"Obviously."

"I do admire your skill in singing of course, but I do have one worry about that, and that is that someday you'll become a conceited jerk who doesn't care about anyone else except yourself and your career."

I laughed. "Don't hold back. Tell me exactly what you're thinking."

She smiled. "I just did."

"Let's see...a conceited jerk. Yeah, that could happen. Here are some signs to look for. If I ever think I'm too busy or too important to help out someone in need. If I ever start refusing callings in the church, that's another clue. If I ever value money over people, then you'll know that I'm on my way to becoming a selfish jerk. If I no longer want to be a disciple of Jesus Christ, then we'll both know I'm in trouble. So when that happens, you tell me what you see and I'll make some course corrections."

She sighed. "I worry that marriage is going to be a lot more complicated than just having you chase me on a mountain trail."

"Speaking of that, I see there's an exit for a trail coming up. Whataya say we take it?"

She fake slugged me. "You can't be serious! You're suggesting this in the middle of our first serious discussion?"

"Yeah, sure. Why not?" I asked with a big smile on my face.

"Okay, you're on but let me warn you, this time I'm not holding back. I'll be going so fast you'll never catch me."

"If I don't catch you, it's your loss."

"How do you figure that?"

"I can't kiss what I can't catch."

"You think I even care about that?" she teased.

"Yeah, we both do."

She nodded. "True but first you'll have to catch me."

"No problem."

"I guess we'll see about that, won't we, Cowboy?"

A short time later I was chasing her up the trail. She did go very fast. Eventually, though, she did let me catch her and we did end up kissing until we saw some other hikers approaching.

"I actually have a question for you," I asked on our way down the trail.

"Okay, what?"

"'Sometimes you playfully slug me on the shoulder. What's that all about?"

"Okay, good question. After my dad and I moved to Cheyenne, I was on the rodeo team. One time a guy on the team tried to kiss me. I slugged him as hard as I could. He never bothered me after that. So I sort of adopted that as a way to keep guys I didn't like away from me. And then, I don't know, it just became a part of who I am. But I can change that."

I nodded. "No, it's okay now that I know where it came from. And, of course, I am much too manly to be bothered by one of your girly punches."

She laughed. "Yeah, right." And then she hit me as hard as she could on my shoulder.

"Ouch!!" I complained. But then I started laughing and she did too.

We continued on our way back down the trail.

"Preparing to get married is a lot harder than I ever thought it would be, isn't it?" she asked.

"Yeah, it is."

She reached for my hand. "Did you ever think that following me up a mountain trail would end up changing your life?"

"No, I never did." I paused. "Now I feel like I wasn't really alive until you came into my life."

"That's the way I feel too. I don't know if I've ever told you this. But I absolutely love your voice. It seems to me now that every other guy I've ever known is still like in fifth grade in terms of his voice. Also, when we're holding each other close, and you say something to me, I can actually feel your voice. I love that too."

I nodded. "Thanks for telling me that. Okay, here's something I've never told you before. Remember the tryouts for *La Bohéme* when you showed up unexpectedly, and how surprised I was. Now wherever I am, I keep hoping you'll surprise me again. I mean like in my American History class, I keep expecting you to show up and sit with me so we can quietly mock what my instructor says."

"Give me the class schedule and I'll come sometime after the opera closes."

"That'll be great," I said. "My life is so dull without you. It's like soup without salt or pumpkin pie without whipped cream."

She laughed. "I'll take that as you being romantic, but of course it could just be that you're hungry."

"Hungry for you," I teased.

She started laughing. "Oh, that is so cheesy."

"I like cheese."

We made it to her pickup. A short time later we were back on the road again.

I leaned over to kiss her cheek but since she was driving she pushed me away. "Sir, do not distract the driver," she said. "Okay this is one I don't want to elaborate on, but one time I had a very romantic dream about us. That is all I care to say at this time."

"You know what? I think we're in love," I said.

"It's true. We are. For sure. So let's get married."

"Let's do." I sighed. "But first t we have to get through *La Bohéme*."

    *   *   *

Two weeks later on a Wednesday *La Bohéme* opened and continued until Saturday night. There were two performances scheduled for Saturday, one in the afternoon and the other at night.

My mom flew out for our first performance. Afterwards she told me how much she loved it. She spent a few hours with Mandy and me that night and the next day she left to go back home. We were so behind in our classes that we couldn't even take her to the SLC airport, but she told us not to worry about it, and ended up taking the shuttle.

Four hours before the Saturday night performance, our director told us that Elizabeth wasn't feeling well, and that Mandy would have to play the part of Mimi for that performance. I later found out that Elizabeth wasn't actually sick and did this because she knew we'd both love the experience, and also because her family and friends had already seen it.

I knew this would be a challenge for Mandy, so I wanted to assure her she could do it, but at first I couldn't find her. Finally I found her in a practice room. There was a bunch of tissues crumpled on the floor next to her chair.

"You okay?" I asked.

She shook her head. "No."

I sat down next to her on a piano bench.

"I'm so nervous," she said in a whisper. "What if I make a mistake?"

"Don't worry. We'll all cover for you. I make mistakes every night but others in the cast cover for me. That's what we do for each other. C'mon, the opera is three hours long so, after a while, the audience isn't paying that much attention anyway so don't worry about it."

"I'm not really a singer."

"No, you actually are. I understand that it's not your first love but you are a singer."

"What if I forget the lyrics to one of the songs?" she asked.

"Okay, I'm going to tell you a trade secret you must never reveal to anyone, okay?"

"I promise."

I reached for her hand. "If you can't remember the lyrics, just do the melody and sing this, 'Dove posso trovare un buon posto per mangiare?" And then just keep singing that phrase or even single words from it to match with the music. Keep doing that until you come to a part you remember."

I helped her practice the emergency phrase until she had it down.

"What does it mean?" she asked.

"It means 'Where can I find a good place to eat?'"

Mandy couldn't stop laughing. "That makes no sense!"

"The reason it works is that most people in the audience don't know Italian. Some know Italian but they'll be sleeping. Others will be focused on their phones. Some won't care what you sing or do because they'll be so focused on how beautiful you are. So bottom line, just keep going and don't panic. This thing is three hours long. Nobody will be paying attention to every word you sing."

She stood up and gave me a hug. "That helps. Thank you."

"You're welcome. Don't worry about this. You'll do great. Just enjoy it."

She nodded. "Could you give me a priesthood blessing?"

"Yes, of course. I'd be happy to do that."

So I gave her a blessing. As I was doing it, I wondered when we were married how many times in the future I'd give her a blessing when she was going through a hard time. I hoped I would always be worthy to do that for her.

She seemed much more relaxed after that.

And, actually, once we got started, it was a great experience for both of us. As far as I could tell, she didn't make any mistakes. I did, of course. But as Mandy often says, this wasn't my first rodeo. So I was able to keep going.

After the performance, when it was time for us to take a bow, we did that and then threw our arms around each other and kissed.

It was a perfect moment for us and for the audience.

On Sunday we went to church but after it was over, we were both so tired that we each went back to our apartments and slept for several hours.

Next week we each worked hard trying to get caught up in our classes. It wasn't until Wednesday night that we spent any time together.

On Sunday after church, we started weekly meetings with our bishop. He told us he liked to meet with couples who were engaged to help us stay worthy for a temple wedding. We appreciated knowing he would check up on us each week. He also gave us some guidelines to follow.

Also on that Sunday, Mandy invited me to have dinner at their apartment. When we were eating dessert, Sara asked Mandy, "How did you get to be such a good singer?"

"Davey taught me. Oh, by the way, Davey, I've never shown this to you before, but come over and touch my stomach."

Sara threw up her hands. "Oh, good grief, can't you two ever leave each other alone! This is Sunday in case you didn't know!"

"This is only about singing," I said.

"Yeah, right!" Sara complained. "I knew it would be a mistake to invite you over for dinner."

"You can touch my stomach if you want!" Monica eagerly told me.

"Uh, maybe later. Right now we want to show you something. Okay, Mandy, do your thing."

She took a deep breath and then slowly let the air out. "Come here, Sara," I said. "The next time she does this, touch her stomach right here."

Sara did what I asked. "Oh my gosh! That is so amazing."

"Can I touch your stomach too?" I asked Mandy.

She nodded and repeated the exercise.

"Wow, you've made such great progress! Good diaphragm! Monica, come here and see what we're talking about."

Pretty soon I had us all standing in a circle doing exercises to strengthen our diaphragms.

Sara apologized for thinking the worst about us.

"Thank you for saying that, Sara," I said. "How are things going with you?"

Sara shrugged. "Okay, I guess. Except I have no guy friends. I go to dances but nobody ever asks me to dance. Do you have any advice for me?"

"Well, not much," I said." You're totally beautiful and you're very smart."

"But what?"

I sighed. "Take off your glasses for just a minute." She did so. "What do you think, Mandy?"

"I actually think it's better without the glasses."

"Me too," I said. "The next time you go to a dance, try it without glasses and see if it makes any difference."

"All right, I will."

"Can you help me too?" Monica asked me.

"In what way?" I asked.

"I want guys to notice me. Can you give me some advice?"

"Well, you know, I'm no expert on things like this. If you want to sing better though, I could help you with that."

"Please, just something."

I sighed. "Mandy, help me out here."

"There's a ward service project this Saturday at some widow's home. What could Monica do that would get some guy's attention?"

"What kind of a service project?" I asked.

"We're going to clean her house," Mandy said." She can hardly walk. Our high councilman knows her and suggested we help."

I nodded. "Okay, Monica, suppose there's a guy washing a window. You walk up and watch for a while, and then say, 'You missed a spot!' Say it with a big grin on your face."

"You're saying that by criticizing his work, he'll like that?" Monica asked.

"If he gets mad, just walk away. He's not worth being your friend. But if he smiles and stops working, keep talking with him. Keep it light and fun and then just see where that goes. If nothing happens, try it with another guy."

Not too much happened for Monica at the service project with that approach, but by the time she'd done it a few times, she could see it wasn't that hard to get a conversation going with a guy.

Three weeks later Sara was seeing a guy. By that time she'd gotten herself contacts. Because of that Sara was no longer always mad at me.

One day Mandy surprised me by showing up to my American History class. She sat next to me. "This is my first time to come to class. Have I missed anything?"

"Well, we've had two exams already, and we usually turn in a written assignment each week."

She did her pouty face. "That is so unfair," she complained.

"I agree. Our teacher should have called you and invited you to come to class, maybe even called you every morning to wake you up so you wouldn't be late."

"That's right. He should have done that."

"I know it's not the same as coming from him, but I personally would like to welcome you to class." I held her hand.

She gave me a big smile. "Wow, you are glad I came, aren't you?"

I nodded. "I find I learn more if I'm holding hands with a girl during a lecture."

"But you don't even know my name, do you?"

"No, but that's never stopped me before."

She laughed. "Well, okay, let's try it."

We had a great time although I have no idea what the lecture was about.

*   *   *

Two days before Thanksgiving, Mandy and I got in her pickup heading for her home in Wyoming, for me to ask her dad's permission to marry his daughter. To complicate matters even more. my mom was flying out for a couple of days to be with us all over Thanksgiving.

We ran into a snow storm on the way, which meant we wouldn't make it to the airport at Jackson Hole in time to pick up my mom. Mandy phoned her dad and asked if he could pick her up. He said he'd be glad to do that.

The snow storm was brief, so an hour later we were able to pick up our speed. Once in Wyoming, Mandy drove fifteen miles an hour over the speed limit.

I warned her about it and she said, "Don't worry about it."

Half an hour later we were pulled over by the highway patrol.

"Oh, Officer, I'm so sorry. I was speeding, wasn't I? Thank you so much for pulling us over. My fiancé and I were so involved in planning our wedding that I must have forgotten to look at the speedometer."

"I'm going to have to give you a ticket."

"Yes, of course, Officer, I completely understand," Mandy said. "My dad raised me to always honor and respect the Wyoming Highway Patrol."

"He did?"

"Oh, yes. Probably because he often works with them."

"In what way?" he asked.

"Well, actually, he's the Wyoming Attorney General."

The officer stopped writing and looked at her last name on the drivers' license, nodded and handed it back to her. "Just keep your speed down now from now on, okay?"

"I will do that! And thank you so much for your kindness!"

As we pulled away, I said, "I think he should have given you a ticket."

"That never happens to me in Wyoming."

An hour later as we pulled onto the gravel road leading to their small ranch, Mandy said, "I hope my dad is not too frustrated with your mom."

As we drove down the gravel road leading to their house, we saw her dad chasing my mom with a pistol in his hand.

"We've got to save your mom!" she yelled. A few seconds later we heard a shot ring out. "Oh, no! My dad just shot your mom!"

"Why would he do that?" I asked.

"Are you kidding me? She'd drive anyone crazy!" she complained.

"But she hasn't been here long enough for your dad to want to take her out!"

And then we heard another shot being fired. "What's that about?" I asked.

"Well, I'm not sure but I can tell you this. When my dad's hunting, if the first shot only wounds the animal, he'll finish it off with a second shot. That way the deer or elk or whatever doesn't suffer so much. He's very humane that way."

"Are you saying your dad just killed my mom? What is wrong with you people here in Wyoming?" We parked and ran down the trail to find my mom.

After about two minutes, we heard someone coming our way.

"We should hide in case my dad decides to take you out too," Mandy said to me.

We hid behind some trees. We watched in shock as her dad and my mom, their arms draped around each other's shoulders, each of them with a pistol in their hand, walked past us.

"Sorry," Mandy said. "This was just a game they were playing,"

"My mom does not play games that involve both running and guns! She's opposed to both."

"My dad and I used to do this when I was a kid. It helped improve my hunting skills. We called our game 'I'm coming to get you!'"

"You and your dad did this with real bullets?"

"Of course not! It's like laser tag."

"Then why did you make me think your dad was hunting my mom?"

"Well, mostly because of my experience with her. Sorry I over-reacted," she said. "When I saw my dad chasing your mom, because of how difficult a woman she is, I naturally thought he'd be chasing her to kill her."

"I can't believe my mom agreed to do this," I said.

"I'll tell you what I can't believe," Mandy said. "I can't believe your mom is wearing my jeans and one of my sweatshirts. I would have thought they'd be too small for her to get into them."

"Maybe you're not as skinny as you think you are."

She shoved me backwards.

"What?" I asked.

"You figure it out!"

We caught up with our parents just before they entered the house.

We each hugged our parent, and gave an awkward hello to the other's parent.

Mandy's dad was over six foot tall with mostly brown hair with a little gray mixed in. He was wearing jeans and a long sleeved flannel shirt. What was most impressive though was what he didn't have. He didn't have a pot belly or bald spots like most men his age.

Because of his appearance, it was easy to think of him as just another cowboy. I had to remind myself though that he'd been a successful corporate lawyer before coming to Wyoming with Mandy, and now was the Wyoming Attorney General.

He and I briefly smiled when we shook hands but there wasn't much friendliness there. It was more like we had to fake it so Mandy wouldn't get mad at either one of us.

"So, Mom, you two were playing a game?" I asked.

"Yes, and I totally wasted him!" my mom said with a huge grin on her face.

"She did! She took me out!" Mandy's dad said.

"So the second shot we heard was you taking him out?" I asked my mom.

"Yes, it was!" She bragged. "Let me tell you how I did it! First I set my phone on the ground, not too far from the house. Then I ran inside and called my own number. Robert heard my phone ringing and headed for the sound. Just before he got to my phone, I stepped outside and blew him away!"

"Nice job!" Mandy's dad said. "Very clever! I'm so impressed!"

He turned to me. "I've been looking forward to meeting you to see if there's any truth to all the good things that Mandy's said about you." He paused. "She exaggerates a lot sometimes."

"It's also hard for me to believe all the great things she's said about you as well." It was only after I'd said it that I realized that probably wasn't a good way to win him over. "When we first pulled in and I saw you chasing my mom with a gun, I was really worried," I said.

"Your mom was never in any danger," he said.

"I know that now. Mom, you never even let me have a toy pistol when I was growing up, so why did you ever agree to some dumb game like this?"

"My flights were long and I needed some exercise," she said. "Besides, Robert said he thought I'd enjoy it, and I did!"

I couldn't let that go. "Mom, is it really a good thing for you to be running through the woods in your condition? You know what your doctor says."

She laughed. "My doctor is an idiot!"

"She got that from my dad," Mandy said quietly to me. "That's what he always says about his doctor."

We heard a timer go off and her dad said it was time for dinner. And so we went inside to their dining room, had a blessing on the food and then started to eat. It was an interesting menu: no salad, just meat, potatoes and green beans.

I couldn't believe it but my mom was eating almost as fast as Mandy, except, to her credit, she didn't use her sleeve to wipe her mouth like Mandy.

"Clary Berry, would you like some more elk steak?" her dad asked my mom.

"Pile it on, Big Guy!" my mom exclaimed.

I panicked. "This is elk meat? How did the poor animal die?"

"Mandy shot and killed it," her dad said with pride. "One shot and it dropped in its tracks!"

Mandy smiled. "That sure brings back a lot of great memories! The hard part was quartering it and then carrying it to our rig. We had to make two trips and it was over five miles each way."

"What does quartering mean?" my mom asked.

Mandy's dad smiled. "Well, basically, you cut it up into four pieces, leave the guts on the ground and haul the meat out. Oh, we had to make another trip to haul out the head so we could have it mounted on the wall. It's in my study. Remind me to show you."

Mandy, with a big smile on her face, said, "We were totally covered in blood and guts by the time we were done! You remember that, Dad?"

"I do. The weird part was when we stopped for a hamburger. Freaked out the guy who took our order! Good times, right?"

"The best!"

I felt sick to my stomach. I couldn't believe that Mandy was proud of what she'd done.

A few minutes later I leaned over to Mandy and said softly. "They're starting to like each other. We've got to stop this."

"I agree."

"I know what will do it," I said quietly. "Get them arguing about gun control. My mom is totally for it."

Mandy nodded and said, "Dad, David's mom feels that the federal government should impose much stricter gun laws. As one who is a lifelong member of the National Rifle Association and a strong advocate for the constitutionally guaranteed right to bear arms, how would you defend your stand on this issue?"

Mandy leaned over to me and whispered, "This will be great! My dad will have your mom bawling in like five minutes."

"I hope so," I whispered back.

Much to our disappointment, my mom argued her position extremely well. A few minutes into the debate, she said. "Robert, that is simply not true! The Constitution does not, nor has it ever guaranteed citizens the right to own any kind of a weapon they choose. I really can't see how banning assault rifles or rocket propelled grenades is going to impinge on your hunting privileges."

Her dad started laughing. "Way to go, Clary Berry! You're so good at this! Good job!"

"I've always loved a good debate!" my mom said.

Mandy and I leaned into each other. "That didn't work, so what else can we do?" I asked.

"I know. I'll tell her all about my mom," Mandy said softly. "That will make them both feel guilty."

"Perfect!"

While Mandy was gone to get a family photo album, I cut the elk steak into small pieces and buried them under my mashed potatoes. Now all I needed to do was to claim I was allergic to potatoes, although my mom would know that was a lie, but maybe she'd let it go. To compensate I dumped green beans all over the potatoes so I could spend all my time eating them.

Mandy came back and handed my mom a well-worn photo album. "I was thinking you might want to learn more about my mom."

My mom graciously received it. "Oh, thank you! That is so kind of you."

With Mandy standing behind her explaining the significance of each photo, they proceeded through the album.

They were looking at a picture of Mandy's mom as a student at BYU, along with her roommates, when my mom suddenly gasped. "Oh my gosh! I can't believe this!"

"What?" Mandy asked.

She pointed to one of the girls in the photo. "This is me! Your mom and I were roommates for a year at BYU! I loved your mom so much!"

"I thought you looked familiar!" Mandy's dad said. "I think I met you once when I was picking up Marilyn."

"Oh, of course, I remember that now! Marilyn always spoke so highly of you."

"Maybe Marilyn is getting us together so we won't be alone anymore," Mandy's dad said.

"That sounds like something she'd do!" my mom said softly. "She was always looking out for others. Maybe she's doing that now for us."

"Maybe so," Mandy's dad said.

Mandy looked sick. "Excuse me. I need to take a walk." She went outside. I followed her.

She ran up a trail. I tried to keep up with her but she was going too fast. At the top of the hill, I found her resting, trying to catch her breath. I sat down next to her. "You okay?"

She shoved me. "What do you think?"

"You're not okay."

"Your mom and my dad are going to get married because they think my mom set them up. But it gets worse."

"How can it get worse than that?" I asked.

"If they get married, then you and I will become brother and sister! Our wedding announcement will read, 'Mr. and Mrs. Robert Wilson proudly announce the wedding of their daughter Mandy to their son David.' You know those trashy magazines at the checkout counter in stores? We'll both be on the front cover because we'll be both husband and wife and brother and sister! That's what's coming our way!"

I tried to hug her but she pushed me away. "What are you doing? Let's make one thing clear. Hugging and kissing is no longer a part of what we do, okay?"

"Why not?" I asked.

She slugged me. "You are sick and twisted and I want no part of this!" She started back down the trail.

"You realize that we'll never be brother and sister, right?" I yelled after her.

She didn't answer.

By the time I made it down to the house, her dad told me that Mandy had a headache and had gone to bed.

Because I couldn't stand to watch my mom flirt with Mandy's dad, I went to one of the guest rooms and got ready for bed.

About half an hour later, I heard my mom and Mandy's dad close the back door. A short time later I heard an engine start. I looked out the window and watched as my mom and Mandy's dad left on an ATV.

I thought they'd be right back, but after an hour I knocked on Mandy's door.

She came to the door. She was wearing sweat pants from her high school and a University of Wyoming sweatshirt as pajamas.

"What do you want?" she grumbled.

"Your dad and my mom left about an hour ago on an ATV. They haven't come back yet. I'm starting to get worried."

Before she came into the living room, she changed into street clothes. When she came into the living room, she got mad at me for still being in my New York Yankees pajamas, so I went and changed too.

She didn't seem to want to talk to me so I decided to watch one of their movies. Mostly they had old westerns so I picked one and started watching it.

The only thing I did wrong was going into the kitchen where she was making up a batch of cookies. She took it personal when, to lighten things up, I started to mimic some of the cowboy dialogue in the movie. "Howdy, Ma'am. You cooking up some vittles for us?"

She glared at me. "You have no respect for people from Wyoming, do you?"

"I respect you."

"And how can you watch a movie at a time like this?" she raged.

"A time like what? Are you worried our folks had an accident and are hurt?" I asked.

"No, not at all. My dad is very careful and skilled in the outdoors. What I worry about is your mom putting a move on him."

"If anything, it's probably the other way around. What with his cowboy impersonation. I mean, come on, he's from California. So why does he talk like he's some Wyoming cowboy? If you ask me, it's all a big act of his to impress women."

She glared at me. "Go back and watch your dumb movie."

"It's not my dumb movie. It's you and your dad's dumb movie."

She pointed a big spoon at me. "I do not want to talk to you at this time!"

So I went back and continued to watch my movie.

After a few minutes I could smell the cookies and so returned to the kitchen.

"Need any help?"

She glared at me. "I'm not giving you a single cookie."

"You're going to eat them all?"

"Yes, I am. Every single one of them."

"If by accident you dropped one of them on the floor, would you let me have it?"

She shrugged. "No, I wouldn't." A tiny smile snuck out of her otherwise serious expression.

"Why are you so mad at me?"

She sighed. "I'm not mad at you. It's something else. I'll give you the answer in seven more minutes."

"Wow, you guys run a tight ship here, don't you?"

She smiled. "That's when the cookies will be done."

When the cookies were done, she brought in a big tray of cookies and two glasses of milk.

I reached for a cookie.

She stopped me. "You can eat after I've answered your question about why I'm mad."

I respectfully put the cookie back on the tray.

"For a long time," she said, "I hoped my dad would never remarry because I knew whoever it was, she couldn't replace my mom. But the last couple of years I sort of wanted him to remarry because I need a mom in my life to tell me things I could never ask anyone else. I fantasized what kind of a woman she would be. I never imagined she'd be like your mom. And now that I can see what may be coming with my dad and your mom, I don't want to have any part of this. If my dad marries your mom, I still won't have what I've wanted so much for all these years. I want my mom back and I'm not going to even get a suitable substitute for her."

"I understand now. Thank you for telling me."

"I think I can hear our ATV coming."

We turned off the lights and waited for them to walk in. As soon as they did, we turned the lights on. "Do you two have any idea what time it is?" Mandy asked.

"We know it's late."

"If you two just knew how worried we've been!" I complained.

"We can explain," my mom said. "It was such a beautiful night and the moon was shining so bright, I talked your dad into giving me a ride on his ATM."

"Actually it's called an ATV," her dad said.

"Why were you gone so long?" Mandy asked.

"Well, to tell you the truth, we've been talking about the possibility of us getting married sometime."

"Are you both crazy? Why would you do that?" Mandy raged.

"Well, the thing is, we each are starting to have a few medical problems," her dad said.

"Nothing serious of course," my mom added. "It's just that sometimes it would be good if we had someone with us, just in case."

Her dad continued. "If we could each have someone we trusted who cared about us and could look out for us, without being a burden on you two, well, that would be good. Neither of us wants to end up in a rest home or living with you two. While we still can, we both want to travel, to see the world, to have someone who genuinely cares about us. It's too early to tell if this would be a good match, but we'd like to explore that possibility."

Mandy shook her head. "You can't be serious! If you two get married, it will make David and me brother and sister! And that means we can never get married!"

"It does not do that," her dad said. "For example, in the case of Rogers vs. Peterson..."

Mandy stood up. "I do not want to hear any legalese!" she yelled.

"Look, don't worry about us getting married because most likely that will never happen," her dad said.

"That's right. Robert wants to stay in Wyoming, and I can't ever imagine leaving California," my mom said.

Her dad nodded. "Even if we do decide to go ahead with this, it will probably take months to work out all the details."

"You would never sell this place, right?" Mandy asked.

"Not while Dance-A-Lot is still alive. That's a promise."

"Good," Mandy said. "To me he's family. He's the one thing that helped me get through the loss of Mom."

"I know. He's family to both of us," her dad said. "He was like an answer to prayer when we first moved here after your mom died."

"Would you like to meet him?" Mandy asked me.

"Yeah, sure," I said.

"Let's go then," her dad said. Our horses have been a big part of Mandy's and my life since we moved here."

He took us out to the barn, turned on the lights, and we got the tour.

"This is Dance-A-Lot," he said. "We got him when we first moved here. For a long time Dance-A-Lot was her best friend."

Mandy grabbed a carrot and held it in her hand. "Hi, Baby, I'm back. I missed you so much!" With one bite, much of the carrot disappeared. "This is David. He's almost as wonderful as you are except he can't gallop."

She had me put out my hand, put a few sugar cubes in my hand, and told me to hold it out for Dance-A-Lot. "Hold your hand out flat so he doesn't chomp down on your fingers."

I did that and it worked, but then I didn't know what to do with my slobbery hand. I saw a paper towel dispenser and wiped it off with one of the towels.

On our way to the next horse, I started sneezing and couldn't stop.

"Oh, that's just his horse and dog allergy," my mom said.

Mandy's dad shook his head and turned to Mandy. "That's all we need in this family, an opera singer with a horse allergy!"

I couldn't stop sneezing. My mom suggested I go inside, take a shower, and put on different clothes. So that's what I did.

As I was getting dressed, the rest of them came back inside.

I had just opened the door to join them when I heard them praying, and then they all said good night so I just stepped back inside my room and closed the door.

About ten minutes later I knocked on Mandy's door.

"What do you want now?" she snapped when she opened the door.

"I just came up with the perfect solution," I said. "If we get married before my mom and your dad, then, at the time we get married, we will not be step brother and step sister."

"But they will still get married though."

"But then your dad will say, 'This is my daughter and her husband.' And my mom will say, 'This is my son and his wife.' So in either case it's okay."

"So what are you saying?" she asked.

"We just need to get married before they do. So, bottom line, we're still engaged, right?"

"Are we?" she shot back.

I was confused. "I love you,"

"Oh, don't give me that! If you loved me, you'd have eaten the elk steak. Just before I went to bed my dad told me about you cutting it up into little pieces and burying the pieces under your mashed potatoes."

"I kept thinking of Bambi."

She shoved me. "Bambi was a deer not an elk!"

"Oh, right, that's good to know. Maybe next time I'll have some of it."

"You will. I put it in the fridge. You can have it for breakfast."

I winced. "Okay, sure, whatever you say."

She started to close the door. "I'm going horseback riding with my dad in the morning so sleep in as long as you want."

"Uh, just one thing. Could you take a shower after you come back so I won't sneeze when I'm around you?"

She slammed the door in my face.

I got up the next morning just after Mandy and her dad rode away on their horses. I went to the kitchen, found my elk-laced potatoes in the refrigerator, took them outside and buried the mess under a rock, then brought back the container and put it in the sink so it would look like I'd eaten it.

About an hour later I saw Mandy and her dad coming back from their horseback ride. They lingered in the barn to talk. I opened the window of my room to see if I could hear what they were saying. I couldn't so I went outside and moved closer to the barn door until I could hear them.

"Okay, bottom line on why I think this is a bad idea," her dad said. "Number one, the guy has a horse allergy which means he'll never go horse-back riding or hunting with us. Number two, he will never want to eat elk or deer or antelope meat. Think of all the money you're going to waste on buying beef. Number three, if you two do get married, and if everything works out the way he wants, you two will end up in New York City so he can be an opera singer. Do you have any idea what that will be like? No mountains, no elk, no sage brush. The only animals you'll be able to hunt will be rats. If this guy wants to sing for a job, why doesn't he just get a job with the Bar J Chuck Wagon Supper and Night Show? He could sing to his heart's content every night and also maybe learn something useful, like how to cook those great baked beans they have there. And you'd both be nearby, including all my grandkids. So I could teach them all the things I taught you. But if he sticks with this New York City opera plan, you two will never live near here and I'll never get to take my grandkids hunting and fishing and horseback riding."

"But Dad, I love him."

"That doesn't mean there's not someone else you could love just as much. All I'm saying here is don't rush into anything. I mean we got some outstanding young men here. For instance, you used to like Jimmy B. after we moved to Cheyenne, right?"

"Dad, why are you bringing him up? His junior year he got a girl pregnant and they had to get married."

"I know but they're divorced now so he's available. You remember what a good calf-roper he was in high school? He went all the way to nationals two years in a row. He would've have gone three times if he hadn't had to drop out to get a job to support his wife and kid."

"You want me to marry him because he's a good calf roper?" Mandy complained. "And yet you're against Davey just because he's an opera singer? That makes no sense. Besides, I love Davey. He's a returned missionary and he's temple worthy and I bet that's more than you can say about Jimmy B."

"I talked to Jimmy B's home teacher and he told me he's making great progress toward being temple worthy. A guy who's made a few mistakes can always get himself temple worthy. But a guy with a horse allergy is going to have it for the rest of his life. It's something to think about. That's all I'm saying."

"I love Davey and I want to be his wife and have his kids."

"That means I'm not going to have much time with my grandkids."

"We'll come every summer with them. When they're old enough, we might even leave them with you for a week or two."

Her dad sighed. "Okay, I guess that's better than nothing. To think I raised a girl who's going to end up marrying a guy whose main goal in life is to sing opera in New York City and isn't even ashamed of it."

"You should have come to the opera and seen him sing. He's really good."

"Yeah, I would have come to see you two do your thing but at the last minute we had that hostage situation."

"I know. It's okay. We'd better go in."

"Okay, Baby Girl, I'll trust you with this, whatever you decide."

"Thanks, Dad. I love you."

"I love you too. Oh, one thing, I'll fix breakfast."

I hurried back into the house before they came out of the barn, went up to my room and took a shower.

I should have taken a longer shower. When I entered the kitchen, there was nobody else in there except Mandy's dad.

"Great, you're just in time!" he said. "When I got up this morning, I looked in the fridge and saw that you'd eaten the elk steak so I'm making a medley of game meat for you to enjoy. We'll start first with some more elk steak. Let me dish you up a big plate since I know how much you like it."

There were no potatoes to hide the meat under. He sat across the table and watched me eat. While I was eating it, he again told me in great detail about how Mandy had shot it, and then how they'd quartered it and then carried it out to their pickup truck. And then how they'd butchered it together on their kitchen table, the same table I was eating on. I felt sick to my stomach.

"Next on our list is antelope meat," he said. "It has a slightly less wild taste. Tell me what you think."

With some difficulty I finished that. "It's not as bad as the elk," I said.

"Now I'm cooking you up some deer meat. Sometimes we call it venison. I'll just give you half a plate of that."

Bambi, I'm so sorry, I thought.

"Could I please have some toast?"

"Well, you could but I don't want you to fill up with toast. I've still got some pheasant, beaver and squirrel meat I'd like you to try. Not just one squirrel though. About a dozen I'd say. We like to shoot 'em Sundays after church."

Just then Mandy came in. "What's going on?" she asked her dad.

"I'm giving David here a sample of all the game we've shot and killed over the years."

She shook her head. "Dad, don't you have something you need to do now?"

"No, not really."

"Why don't you take David's mom horseback riding?"

He thought about it. "Okay, maybe I will." He left.

She sat down. "Sorry. This is my dad's version of tough love."

"It's okay." I paused. "Could I please have some cinnamon toast and, also, some orange juice?"

"Coming right up."

She also made us some scrambled eggs then sat down with me to eat.

The best thing about the morning was that after the blessing she dumped ketchup on her eggs. I stood up and raised my arms high in the air. "Yes! This is the best day of my life!"

"What are you talking about?"

"You put ketchup on your eggs!"

"Yeah, so?"

"I've gone my whole life secretly buying ketchup and hiding it in my room so I could pour it on my eggs when my mom was gone. Once we're married, I won't have to do that anymore! Can we have eggs the morning after we're married? "

She laughed. "Whatever. You are so weird sometimes."

After breakfast Mandy and I took a hike to the top of a mountain.

We kissed a few times and then she started to point out the scenery in front of us.

I stood a little behind her. Every time she pointed out some interesting geographical feature, it gave me a chance to take in her beauty without making her self-conscious.

She had her hair tied up which gave me a chance to focus on the back of her neck. Not everyone has a beautiful neck but she definitely does.

"This is such a good place to see, you know, things of beauty in nature," I said.

"It really is."

Everything worked great until one time she noticed I wasn't even looking at the lake she was pointing to. "What are you doing?" she asked.

"What do you mean?"

"I'm showing you points of interest and instead of looking at them, you're checking me out?"

"Yeah, pretty much. You're so beautiful! Let me point out a few features I especially appreciate."

She scowled. "You're not going to get weird on me, are you?"

"No. First of all, nature lovers, let us focus our attention on this creature's neck and also the dimple on her right cheek."

I tore off a small branch of a tree to use as a pointer. "Here we see her outstanding dimple. This only shows when this creature is happy or amused. It can be found right here."

She frowned.

"Unfortunately the conditions are not right for her dimple to make its appearance at the present time. So let's move on to the neck."

She shook her head

I continued. "Okay, here's the neck as promised. This creature has an amazing neck. It makes me want to kiss it. Let's ask permission. Beautiful creature, may I kiss the back of your neck?"

She shook her head. "Whatever."

I kissed the back of her neck. "Has anyone ever kissed your elbows?" I whispered in her ear.

She started laughing.

"Ah, nature lovers, we are most fortunate!" I announced "The elusive dimple has made its appearance. Now perhaps we may venture to the eyes of this fascinating creature."

She pushed me away. "Let me do the nature guide thing on you, okay?"

I shrugged. "You know what? I got nothing."

"Hold me in your arms," she said.

I did.

"There's nothing like being held by this creature," she said. "It makes me feel safe and cared about. That's very important to me. This creature is gentle enough to hold a baby and silly enough to play with kids we're going to have, chasing them around the house. With his amazing voice he can pretend to be a bear as he chases them. And yet he's righteous enough to give a priesthood blessing when asked, and kind enough to do my math homework when I'm having a hard day. He's also romantic enough to bring some charm when we're married even when times are tough. When he kisses me, it's a magic time for both of us. I love this creature. He makes me very happy and I'm totally in love with him. And, not only that, this creature can sing! When he sings out here, the birds stop chirping because they want to hear him."

We kissed and it was amazing.

"Let's sing together up here," I suggested.

We sang the duet "O soave fanciulla" from *La Bohéme*. With all that beauty around us and all that beauty from that duet, it was an amazing experience for both of us. And then we sang some church hymns that brought the spirit.

On our way back down to the house, Mandy gave me a hug. "Good luck talking to my dad, Bro. Don't be intimidated by him just because he was a noted attorney in California before we moved here and now is the Attorney General for the State of Wyoming." She said this with a big smirk on her face.

I cleared my throat nervously. "No problem. Piece of cake."

After lunch I met with Mandy's dad to ask his permission to marry his daughter. We met in his study which was a little threatening because it had an elk head, a deer head and a bear hide mounted on the wall. It was like they were trying to warn me to escape while I still had the chance or I'd end up just like them.

"I would like to ask your permission to marry Mandy," I said.

"Does that mean you are asking my permission or that you would like to but you're not man enough to get the job done?" he asked.

"I am asking permission," I said in my deepest most resonant opera voice.

He nodded, then shook his head and sighed. "I always knew this day would come. I've tried to prepare for it but, well, the truth is, this is very difficult for me."

"I understand."

"I doubt if you do, but thanks for saying that. Let me ask you another question. Do you have any kind of a criminal record? You know, like shop lifting, armed robbery, destruction of property, or sexual crimes?"

"No, sir."

"You sure about that? As the Wyoming Attorney General, I can check for criminal records, so you might as well tell me the truth now."

I shook my head. "I've never done anything like that."

"You sure?"

"Yes sir, I'm sure."

"When's the last time you watched pornography?" he asked.

"Never."

"With all due respect, I don't see how that's possible in this day and age. I mean you do watch TV, don't you?"

"Not that much actually."

"What about movies? Have you ever watched an R-rated movie before?"

"No."

"You sure about that?"

"If you don't believe me, why don't you look it up? I'm sure you have records of every movie I've ever watched too, right?" I asked sarcastically.

He glared to me to see if I'd fold. I didn't. Instead I pulled my temple recommend from my wallet and handed it to him. "I'm worthy of this. The way I see it, that's all you need to know about my worthiness."

"When's the last time you went to the temple?"

"Last week."

He nodded. "Okay. Let me move on to some other things then. What are you going to do if your dream of being a big time opera singer doesn't pan out?"

"I'll probably go to graduate school with the idea of teaching in the music department at some university."

"And what if that doesn't work out?" he asked.

"That's not something I worry about. I'm very good at what I do. In that sense, you and I have a lot in common.'

He couldn't decide to get mad at me or not. Finally he nodded. "I like that attitude."

"Are we done here?" I asked.

"We're not done until I say we're done!" he said emphatically.

"Yes, sir."

"What kind of a missionary were you?" he asked.

"Exceptional. If you don't believe me, call my mission president and ask him. Here's his number." I handed him a piece of paper with the number on it.

"Maybe I will. Another question: Are you a hard worker?"

"Yes, I am."

"How is it possible for someone who grew up in San Francisco to work hard? No livestock...no horses...no crops. To me that's an excuse to be lazy."

"We had a garden. My mom kept me busy working on that. And I spent a lot of time on homework."

He got up and paced back and forth. "What you're asking me for is very hard on me. I'm not ready to let her go, and probably never will be." He went to the bookshelf and pulled out a photo album. They contained their wedding pictures.

He pointed at picture of his wife. "Any comments?"

"She looks a lot like Mandy."

"Yeah, she does." He sighed. "After my wife died, I quit my job and we moved here. The only thing that kept me going was that every time I looked at Mandy, I could see features of my wife: her eyes, her smile, her laugh. That kept me going. So what I'm trying to say is this is not just a father's hesitation in having some random guy come and marry his daughter. This is like I'm losing someone who helped me get through the darkest period of my life. This is a big deal and it's going to take me a while to get used to the idea."

"I can see why."

He sighed. "I knew this day would come sometime. And I knew that by sending Mandy to BYU, it meant she might marry someone not from around here. I mean I could have sent her to the University of

Wyoming. But I decided against it because a temple marriage is more important than that some guy knows how to ride a horse."

"I agree."

He sighed. "So, bottom line, if you want to marry my daughter, you have my permission."

I thought about hugging him but decided against it so we shook hands. "Thank you, sir. I'll treat her well."

"You'd better, that's all I can say."

He paused. "While we're here, let me tell you how I got the bear," he said.

"That would be great."

"Okay, this was just outside Yellowstone National Park. I'd tracked him for most of the day."

His story was actually interesting, which was a surprise to me.

"You're not everything I would have liked for a son in law," he said.

"Where am I lacking?" I asked.

He broke into a big grin. "Well, for one thing, you've never shot and killed a bear."

"That's not my fault. I've been hunting them in San Francisco for years, but I never had any luck. There's so few of them around there anymore."

He smiled. "Okay, then, the marriage question is settled. Now it's time for me to help you out a little while you're here. You have no idea how much Dance-a-Lot meant to Mandy after she lost her mom. Sometimes she'd sleep in the barn with that dang horse because it was the only thing that gave her any comfort. So, the way I see it, you've got to go horseback riding with us because that was such an important part of her life growing up. Last night I came up with a plan that might make this possible. Are you willing to try it?"

"Yes sir."

"Okay, this afternoon Mandy, your mom and you and I are going horseback riding. But it's going to be okay. I've got some pills I'll have you take that will keep you from sneezing. Also I'll have you leading us all and going into the wind so you won't be getting anything from the other horses. We'll be out for like half an hour and then we'll hurry back. With any luck, you won't be sneezing, and Mandy will be impressed."

"Thank you. I don't want Mandy thinking it's either me or her horse."

After lunch we did the ride. I didn't sneeze. Mandy was happy. And I owe it all to her dad.

I liked her dad now a lot more than when I first met him.

The best part of our time together over Thanksgiving was seeing our parents happy and enjoying their time together.

The worst part of our time together over Thanksgiving was seeing our parents happy and enjoying their time together.

CHAPTER FOUR

After Mandy and I were done with finals for fall semester, we drove to San Francisco. Her dad flew out the same day. The next day Mandy received her endowment in the Oakland Temple. Her dad and my mom and I were there with her.

The next day, a Saturday, we were married in the Oakland Temple. Our parents, of course, were there with us. While we were still in the temple, my mom and Mandy's dad told us they were not going to be sealed in the temple because they had already been sealed. They were just going to be married civilly. "So our marriage will be for time but not for eternity."

"Are you okay with that?" Mandy asked them.

"Yeah, we both are," her dad said.

That night there was a wedding reception in my home ward. Lots of people came, including Hillary who gave us both big hugs and wished us the best. Some of the guys I'd grown up with in my ward also came. They told Mandy what a good guy I was. I was relieved that none of them mentioned the summer camp Listerine incident.

Mandy and I spent our first night together in a fancy hotel in San Francisco.

I woke up at seven thirty the next morning but Mandy was still asleep. I went to the bathroom and then returned to bed but I wasn't sleepy. I was filled with such gratitude that I knelt at the side of the bed and silently thanked Father in Heaven for blessing me so much by giving me Mandy to be my wife.

She woke up, saw me praying and waited for me to finish.

"Oh, gosh, Davey Boy, you don't have to pay obeisance to me just because of how amazing last night was," she teased.

I tossed a pillow at her. "Are you kidding me? There's no way some hick cowgirl from Wyoming can know what the word obeisance means!"

"What are you talking about?" she complained. "The word obeisance was in our school song in my high school in Cheyenne!"

"I think that is highly unlikely."

She shrugged. "Would I lie to you?" She gave me a big innocent smile.

"Yes, you would. So tell me this. In that school song what word does obeisance rhyme with?" I asked.

"Nuisance, which is what you are now!" She tossed a pillow at me.

And that started a pillow fight.

A few minutes later, still in bed, with our pillows propped up, we talked. "So you were praying, right?" she asked.

"Yeah, I was thanking Father in Heaven for bringing us together," I said.

"I feel that way too."

"And, also, I let Father in Heaven know how grateful I am not to have had any past mistakes. Because of that I couldn't make comparisons to anyone else I might have been with before you. In high school, guys would talk about girls they'd been with and how it was, and sometimes I'd feel like I was missing out on something. I didn't understand this then but now I can see that chastity before marriage is a gift we give to our spouse."

"I totally agree. To associate what we did last night as a married couple with something dirty or bad must be so hurtful to Father in Heaven because He gave intimacy to those who are married. In a way it's his wedding gift to us."

We talked for a few more minutes. And then, because we were hungry, we got dressed and went to the continental breakfast on the first floor.

Besides other things we both got a lot of scrambled eggs. We both poured huge amounts of ketchup on them. "This is like a dream come true!" I said.

She smiled and shook her head. "You are so weird."

Back in our room, she pulled a gift-wrapped package from her suitcase and gave it to me. "This is my special gift to you," she said, handing me the package.

"I didn't get anything for you," I said.

"Relax. This isn't a serious gift."

I opened it. It was a bottle of Listerine.

She shook my hand. "Congratulations! You've won the No More Listerine Award. What I thought we'd do is pour it down the drain a little at a time and celebrate your becoming independent from your mom's interference in your life. Congratulations! Do you have anything to say?"

"I couldn't have done this without you!"

"True. Let the celebration begin!"

We went into the bathroom and opened the bottle. She poured a small amount into a drinking glass and handed it to me. "What experience from your youth, when your mom interfered, would you like to de-celebrate?" she asked.

"Well, of course, her sending me to camp with a bottle of Listerine and making me promise to gargle both morning and night with it."

"Yeah, that was really bad. Okay, go ahead and get rid of it."

I poured the Listerine in the glass into the sink.

She filled the glass again. "What else?" she asked.

"She never bought me a video game. In place of that, she got me a book about chess and sometimes we'd play. For some reason she was very good at that, so I lost every game."

"Poor guy," she said. "Let's get rid of that memory too."

I poured another glass into the sink.

"What else?" she asked.

"My dad had a lot of camping equipment he used whenever the company he worked for had a retreat. He was always going to take me but my mom always had me in some music activity and insisted I couldn't miss a practice. When my dad died, she gave away all the camping gear to some charity. I got none of it."

"Wow, how could she have done that?" Mandy said.

"I know."

We poured another batch of Listerine down the drain. "What else?" she asked.

I paused. "I hate to say this, but in many ways, my mom is a racist. Some of that became a part of me until my mission. So now I feel bad that I held back from making friends in high school with Blacks and Hispanics because I believed what she'd told me. What a wasted opportunity."

The exercise had lost its charm for both of us. Mandy gave me the bottle and asked me to pour it all out. "You're no longer Mommy's obedient little boy, are you?"

"No, I'm not."

"You're your own man now," she said.

I gave her a big hug. "I am. Thank you for helping me to get there. I love you, Mandy."

"I love you too, with all my heart. Okay, let's get out of here and go be a married couple!"

We attended a one o'clock sacrament meeting in the nearest ward. We sat in the back and didn't stay for the other meetings. We were too self-conscious to explain to anyone that we'd just been married.

Later that day we drove to Las Vegas where we stayed the night. The next day we did the tourist thing .That night we went to Opera Las Vegas. I enjoyed it tremendously, and Mandy enjoyed her nap during the second act.

The next day we drove to Zions National Park and stayed the night in a motel.

Early the next day we did a little hiking and then drove to the SLC airport where we parked Mandy's pickup. And then we took a flight to Cheyenne.

That night there was a reception in the ward building where Mandy and her dad attended after they'd moved there when her dad became attorney general.

Lots of legal professionals showed up for the reception as well as some of Mandy's Young Women leaders and her former bishop and his wife.

I also got to meet Jimmy B., the guy Mandy's dad had suggested she marry instead of me.

"I understand you're an awesome calf roper," I said to him.

"I used to be, but not so much now."

When we had a minute, Mandy asked, "How did you know he was a calf roper?" Mandy asked.

I then remembered I'd heard her dad talk about him when I was eavesdropping to their conversation in the barn.

"I heard your dad talk about him," I said, hoping she wouldn't ask for more details.

I felt guilty so that night told her the truth. She gave me a hug and told me she appreciated my honesty.

We stayed that night in her bedroom in their Cheyenne home. As we got into bed, she smiled and said, "Well, this is a dream come true--in my own bed with my very own husband."

"Yeah, great, but do all your stuffed animals have to be in bed with us too?" I asked.

"Not anymore." She pushed all the stuffed animals on the floor. "You know why? Because you've become my favorite stuffed animal!"

"I'm going to take that as a compliment."

"Oh, Baby, it is!"

Early the next morning there was a knock at the door.

"Come in," Mandy said. I looked at her like she was crazy because we were in bed together, but then I reminded myself it was okay now that we were married.

Her dad opened the door. "David, your mom and I have decided to get married today by a justice of the peace. We're tired of waiting, and, besides, we're not going to get married in the temple. And we're tired of going to receptions so we're just going to get married. So I need you both to get up and get dressed. We need to get this done before you two head back to Utah."

"Can you get a license that fast?" Mandy asked.

"Hey, I'm the state attorney general. I'm pretty sure I can make that happen."

Two hours later they got married. We gave them each a hug and wished them well.

That afternoon we flew back to Salt Lake City and then took the shuttle so we could get to her pickup in the airport parking lot.

As we walked to her pickup, I asked, "You like my rig?" I asked in what I hoped was a cowboy accent.

"I do!" she said, sounding like a groupie. "You must be a real cowboy!"

"Why yes, I am, Ma'am," I said in my best cowboy drawl. "Almost every day I get on my horse and call out 'Get along little dogie!'"

"How exciting! Can you give me a ride in your rig?" she teased.

"You betcha! I'd actually like to drive you where we can be totally alone, just you, me and the dogies."

"Oh, please do," she said with a big grin on her face.

We drove to Provo to our married student apartment. There were no dogies, but she didn't seem to mind.

*   *   *

Life was good for us at BYU except we had very little money.

The arrangement between my mom and me was for her to pay my tuition for winter semester and our living expenses for January. Mandy asked her dad to pay her tuition for winter semester. After that we'd take over and pay our own way.

Because we had to save money, we both got jobs on campus. I worked mornings on a custodial crew. I got up at two forty five, started work at three a.m. and worked until seven. On Saturdays I worked until eleven because we had to set up for campus wards that would be meeting in the building the next day.

Mandy worked in the girls' locker room handing out gym clothes. She started at four in the afternoon and finished by ten thirty at night.

At any hour of the day one of us could barely stay awake. On Sundays after church we'd have a bowl of soup and take long naps just trying to catch up on our sleep.

Don't get me wrong. We were very happy. It was just a tired happy.

My mom called every week. She always asked if Mandy was pregnant yet. We came to not only dread the question but also to resent her detailed and personal suggestions. They were not only embarrassing but also quite inappropriate. "David, I'm sending you some wheat germ which I'd like you to have for breakfast every morning. Also, when you use a lap top, make sure you don't put it on your lap because that could reduce your count."

That was unbelievably awkward. "Thanks, Mom. Well, I got to go to work now. Bye."

Because we were in a campus ward, many of us were newly married, which meant we didn't have that much interest in getting together socially with anybody. That tended to isolate everyone but nobody complained.

We were both in our sophomore year at BYU. Because of our work schedule, the thought of living this way for two more years was very depressing.

"We need scholarships," Mandy said, "even if it's at another university. Do they have those for opera majors?"

"I'm not sure."

"Well how about if you start looking? And I'll see what I can find for me."

"Yeah, sure, good idea."

And so I did begin. With each application I sent a flash drive featuring me on stage singing from *La Bohéme*.

On the third Saturday in January, our parents made a surprise visit to us at eleven thirty in the morning. They'd just been to a conference in D.C. for state attorney generals, but had decided to stay over a couple of nights in SLC and visit with us before they flew out to San Francisco. (They had decided to spend winters in California and summers in Wyoming.)

I had just finished my custodial work on campus and had just climbed into bed. I'd been up since two thirty that morning.

When they knocked at the door, I went to see who it was.

"Surprise!" my mom said.

"Hi, Mom. Hi there." I couldn't say dad because he wasn't my dad.

"You're still in your pajamas this time of day?" she asked.

"Yes."

"You have New York Yankee pajamas?" my father-in-law asked.

I was in no mood for this. "Why don't you come back in a few hours? We need to catch up on our sleep."

"Why's that?" he asked.

"I just got home from my custodial job. And Mandy worked until about eleven last night. We actually spend very little time together."

"That might explain why Mandy isn't pregnant yet," my mom said, looking at my father-in-law.

That made me mad but I didn't say anything. "Come back about two this afternoon. We'll both be wide awake by then."

I closed the door on them and then got back in bed.

"Who was that?" Mandy asked.

"My mom and your dad. I sent them away and told them to come back at two o'clock."

"But that won't give us enough time with them. I have to go to work today at three."

"Oh, yeah, sorry," I said.

"I'll call Ally and ask if she can fill in for me," she said.

She called and made arrangements to get off work that day.

"What are they doing here?" she asked.

"I don't know."

"You sent them away?"

"Yeah, I did. I told them we never get enough sleep."

She sighed. "I see." She went back to bed with me.

Five minutes later she got up.

"What are you doing?" I asked.

"We need to clean up for our folks," she said.

"Are you serious?"

"We can't let them see our place like this."

"Why not?"

She sighed. "Because my dad will blame it on you, and your mom will blame it on me."

I sighed. "All right. I'll get up too."

The first thing I did was to take the stack of empty pizza boxes in the kitchen and throw them in the dumpster. Next I vacuumed our old carpet. It actually looked better before I vacuumed it because the dirt had been hiding how worn the carpet was.

Then we washed the dishes. We always tried to do that at least once a week, usually on a Saturday.

We also pulled out the bag where we'd been shoving all the vitamins and other pills my mom had been sending us so we'd both be healthy enough for Mandy to get pregnant.

"Have you actually taken any of these?" Mandy asked me.

"No, how about you?"

"No. That means we need to take one or two of them in case they ask and then we need to say we think they're really helping."

Which we did.

"What else do we need to do?" I asked.

"You need to take a shower after having worked, right?"

"Yeah."

"Okay. You take a shower while I make our bed. And then I'll take a shower while you clean out the refrigerator."

I paused. "What exactly does it mean to clean out the refrigerator?"

"Throw everything out that's in there, except for the milk, the butter and the picante sauce." And then she sighed.

"What's wrong?" I asked.

"I'm sorry I'm such a lousy housekeeper. I grew up with my dad in charge. We kept things mostly clean, but your mom is going to find things wrong that I would never think of."

"Like what?"

She shrugged. "That's just it. I don't know."

After we'd finished cleaning up, we both took naps.

A little after 2 o'clock, our parents showed up. We gave them a tour of the apartment.

"Very nice," my mom said. "You two keep it up so nice."

"I especially like this year-old calendar on your wall," Mandy's dad said. "You don't get that many good pictures of red dogwood trees. I'm sure that's why you keep it here."

Truth is we'd never noticed the calendar. "Yes, we chose it because we liked it so much," I said.

"So time stands still here, right?" my mom said. I could tell she couldn't believe we'd have a calendar on the wall that was over a year old.

"Oh, that's very funny!" Mandy said.

They both wanted to see the campus, which took forever because they had to each tell us things that had happened to each of them while students there. Also, my mom kept talking about all she'd seen in the museums she'd gone to while Mandy's dad was in his meetings in D.C.

"We'd like to take you two out for dinner," my mom said.

"Great!" Mandy said.

"And then maybe a movie after," my mom said. "You probably don't go out much, do you?"

"Not much," I said. "And naturally we appreciate the offer but I have to get up at six in the morning so I need to go to bed early."

"Tomorrow is a Sunday. Why do you need to get up so early?" Mandy's dad asked.

"I'm the bishop's executive secretary and he needs me to be with him for all his meetings on Sunday."

"I home teach an eighty year old with a more active social life than you two."

"It's not a bad thing they're trying to spend more time together in bed," my mom said.

Mandy frowned. "We understand you two want grandchildren and you don't have any other kids that can make that happen. I'm sure we'll have them sometime, so just relax and let it happen when it happens."

"Don't wait too long, that's all I'm saying," my mom said. "I only had one." And then she sighed as if I hadn't been exactly what she was looking for in a son.

That made Mandy mad. "Careful! That one son of yours is now my husband. And I think he's amazing."

"Oh, yes, of course. I'm very grateful to at least have had him. But still..."

"Just drop it, okay?" Mandy said. "Well, enough of this. Take us out to eat. That'll be great as long as we're back by seven thirty."

We ate at a restaurant with very slow service. I had a hard time staying awake until the food came.

They finally talked us into going to a movie with them.

During the movie, Mandy reached for my hand. "I don't care what your mom says," she whispered. "There's nobody I'd rather be married to than you."

"Thank you. I feel the same way about you."

"We're the only ones we need to please, not my dad, not your mom, just us."

"I agree." I yawned. "I'm so tired. You think it's okay if I take a nap?"

"Yeah, sure, go ahead. I might do the same."

Mandy was awake the first time I woke up. Fearing my mom would ask me a bunch of questions to punish me for falling asleep, "What's happened so far?" I whispered to Mandy.

"You know the guy with the scar on his face? Well, he just got run over by a bus."

"Okay, good. Anything else?" I asked.

"That's all I remember. I fell asleep just after you did, and just woke up."

I sighed. "So all we got is a guy being run over by a bus?"

"Yeah, pretty much."

"I hope that's very significant to the plot," I whispered.

"Me too."

"Okay, well, I'm going to see if I can get some more sleep," I said.

"Me too."

"I'm going to lean forward with my chin on my hand like I'm totally interested in what's going on," I said.

"I think I'll do that too."

"Perfect."

The next thing I remember is Mandy touching my hand. "It's over."

"How did it turn out?"

"I have no idea. I just woke up, but the music at the end seemed real up-beat."

Our folks didn't say anything until we made it to the car and were on our way to our apartment.

"Well, did you two get anything out of this?" my mom asked.

"Oh, yeah, are you kidding?" I said. "I especially liked the part where that guy got run over by the bus. That was really good."

"That had nothing to do with the main plot," her dad said.

"I know that, but I...I don't know...I just felt sorry for the poor guy."

He shook his head.

My mom wasn't happy with us either. "We thought that if we went out of our way to provide you both with a little entertainment that you'd be grateful enough to enjoy it, and not sleep through the whole thing."

"We did enjoy it. It's just that theater seats are so comfortable," Mandy said.

"And the smell of popcorn, especially in a movie theater," I added, "always puts me to sleep."

"And of course being with you two is always...uh...," Mandy added.

"A challenge?" I whispered in Mandy's ear.

Mandy poked me. "A treat. Also, we enjoy having you two critique how we're living our life and, you know, good stuff like that."

I whispered in her ear. "I can't believe you said that."

"Oh one thing we haven't told you," Mandy's dad said. "In May we're flying to Labrador for a two week visit."

"Labrador? Oh, I've heard so much about Labrador!" Mandy said.

"What have you heard?" her dad asked.

Long pause. "Well... where can I begin?" Mandy said. "I've heard that it's beautiful, what with...you know... the scenery and everything,"

I snickered. She poked me in the stomach.

"They have a lot of fjords in Labrador," her dad said.

I whispered in her ear. "Give it up. You're not going to pull this off."

She shook her head. "I totally got this." Ignoring my advice, she said, "Oh, yes, fjords! If you ask me, we could use a lot more fjords here in the United States."

"You don't even know what a fjord is, do you?" I whispered.

She didn't answer the question. "How long will you be gone?" she asked her dad.

"Ten days," her dad said.

"Sounds like fjord heaven to me!" I said.

At which Mandy and I both started laughing.

A short time later her dad pulled into our driveway.

"We'll send you pictures," my mom said.

"That will make it be just like we're there with you!" Mandy said.

My mom wanted to hug us but Mandy's dad had been offended by our treating his love of fjords with disrespect. "We need to go!" he said.

I couldn't leave things this way. After I got out of the car, I walked over to the driver's side. Mandy's dad rolled down his window.

"I apologize for our behavior at the movie. I only had four hours of sleep last night. And Mandy didn't have much more than that. When we get tired, we laugh at anything. Also, I'm sorry we made fun of your trip to Labrador. Please forgive us. We're just so tired."

He nodded. "Don't worry about it. We'll go so you two can get some sleep."

"Thank you. And thank you for stopping by. Please send us pictures of your visit to Labrador. We will enjoy looking at them."

"We'll do that," he said and then they left.

As they drove away, Mandy kissed me on the cheek. "Thank you for apologizing to my dad for us."

"No problem."

I had Mandy brush her teeth in the bathroom while I did the same at the kitchen sink. That gave me three more minutes of sleep, which I so desperately needed.

     *   *   *

In mid-March we found out that Mandy was pregnant.

My mom and her dad were ecstatic. "I knew those pills would help!" my mom said.

Her dad's response was, "Way to go, you two!"

A few days later we received another box of pills for Mandy to take. She started taking some of them.

We were, of course, very excited and happy.

Mandy cut down her hours of work, which meant I needed to work more. But that was okay. I was willing to do that.

I started giving voice lessons to kids. I made up a flyer and every Saturday would go door to door, leaving my flyer, and for those interested, would sing to the parents at their front door.

It's amazing how few parents want their kids to learn to sing, but I did get a few to agree to have me come once a week and work with one of their kids, or in a few cases, with one of the parents themselves.

What I was getting for thirty minute voice lessons was much better than what I got being a custodian.

On the second Friday in May, I'd made arrangements to go with Alex, a twelve year old boy, to a music festival in Salt Lake City where he would sing. It was to be an all-day event.

Alex's mom drove. We left at nine in the morning.

At two o'clock, Mandy called. "I need you here now. I'm spotting and I'm worried. I'm going to go to the hospital to get myself checked out. I'm so worried. I need you here with me."

"Okay, I'll see if I can get Alex's mom to take me back to Provo."

I asked Alex's mom if she could either drive me back or let me borrow her car because my wife was worried about having a miscarriage.

"Alex will be singing in fifteen minutes. After he's done, we'll all go back."

"I need to go now!"

"I'll take you back after Alex sings. You can't expect any more from me than that."

I went out into the parking lot. When I saw someone leaving, I'd hurry over to them. "I need a ride to Provo right away. Are you going that way?"

After four no's I changed what I said. "My wife is about to have a miscarriage. I need to get to her as soon as I can. Is there any chance you could give me a ride to the hospital in Provo?"

Three more no's.

By this time fifteen minutes had passed, so I went in to see how soon it would be before Alex sang.

"He's the next one," his mom said.

The judge stood up. "We'll be taking a ten minute break now."

I ran over to him. "Please don't take a break now! I need to get to my wife in Provo and I'm stuck here without a car. Alex Remington is the next singer. I'm with him. Can't you just let him sing and then take a break?"

"Sorry. I really need to use the restroom."

After three minutes, I stormed into the restroom. "How long does it take to go to the bathroom?" I yelled.

"Longer if you've had an operation," the judge in the booth said.

"Please hurry up!"

"I will. I'm almost done."

I came out of the restroom and called Mandy. No answer. I left a message. "I've been trying to get a ride back but haven't had any luck, but we'll be leaving in like five minutes. Love you."

Twenty minutes later we were on the road back to Provo.

In the hospital at the nurse's station, not far from where they were keeping Mandy, I was told she'd had a miscarriage.

I entered her room. She was sleeping.

I sat down and waited.

A couple of hours later she woke up. She looked at me and said, "You didn't come."

"I tried as hard as I could."

"You didn't come."

"No, I'm so sorry."

"I lost my baby," she sighed.

I nodded. "The nurse told me."

"You didn't come."

I sighed. "I couldn't get anyone to bring me back here."

"I needed you to be here with me, but you didn't come."

"I know. I'm so sorry. I tried so hard to get here."

She nodded and turned so she wasn't looking at me anymore.

A short time later she fell asleep.

I called and told my mom and her dad the news.

"Was she taking all the pills I sent her?" my mom asked.

"Mostly."

"Well I guess you can see now what mostly did for her."

"I can't talk now, Mom. Bye."

There was nothing I could do but wait and see if Mandy would ever trust me again.

CHAPTER FIVE

Mandy spent the night in the hospital. The next day she was released. Not long after we'd entered our apartment, her dad called Mandy. "Would you like me to come and help out?" he asked.

"No, Dad. We're doing okay."

"What about David's mom?" he asked. "She'd love to come and help out."

"No. The Relief Society in our ward, along with Davey, will take good care of me."

"Are you sure? She really wants to come."

"And I'm grateful for that but honestly, Dad, I'll get more sleep if she's not here."

He sighed. "I understand," he said. A short time later, he told her he loved her and then hung up.

She slept for a few hours and then woke up and asked for a bowl of chicken noodle soup. "Get Campbell's. That's what my dad and I ate a lot after we moved to Wyoming. I guess it reminded us of my mom. She used to give that to us on rainy days."

I bought ten cans. By the time I returned, she was sitting on the couch in our living room. She saw me unloading the cans. "Why did you get so much?" she asked.

"I didn't want to run out."

"You think I'll never recover from this?" she asked.

This was like walking through a mine field. "No, you will, eventually," I said.

Apparently I'd made her mad using the world eventually, because by the time I'd warmed up the soup, she told me she didn't want it anymore.

"Maybe you'll change your mind," I said, setting it on a coffee table in front of the couch.

"I don't care about the stupid soup, okay? Don't you get it? We've lost our baby girl! Have you ever thought about what she would have been like?"

I sighed. "I've been so busy lately."

"All my dreams and hopes about her have vanished! Disappeared. Gone forever. Do you even remember what we were going to call her?"

"We talked about several names for her or him."

"I was leaning toward April."

"Oh."

"Everyone loves April," she said.

I had to stop and think about everything I said in case it might upset her all over again. "That's true. April is a very good month," I said.

"Have you ever imagined how it would be to hold your daughter in your arms and sing her to sleep?"

The truth is I hadn't done that because she wasn't due for months. "Of course I have," I lied.

"What songs were you going to sing to her?"

I hesitated too long. "The usual songs you sing to a baby."

"And now what do we do?" she asked.

"We just move on."

For some reason that made her mad. "So you, being a man, are just going to cross this loss off your list of goals and move on, right?"

"April was never born. What do you want me to do?"

"I want you to take some of the intense loss I'm feeling! She was in my body. I felt her wanting to come out and be with us. You're tossing this off like it has as much significance as if you'd bought a lottery ticket and ending up not winning. So you just shrug, throw the ticket away and continue on with your life, right?"

I sighed. "Look, I'm sorry you had a miscarriage, but even if I'd been at the hospital, I couldn't have stopped it. What do you want me to do?"

"I want you to grieve the loss of our daughter! She was going to be your daughter too! Why can't you mourn with me on our loss?"

And with that she broke down sobbing.

I didn't know what to do. I sat there for like ten minutes and then asked, "What do you want me to do?"

"I want you to get out of here! Let me suffer here without you!"

"Do you want the soup or not?"

"No, I don't want the stupid soup!! Just get out of here and leave me alone!"

So I took an hour walk. She never did eat the soup. When I came back, I could see she'd made herself a peanut butter sandwich and eaten half of it.

I hadn't planned to go to work in the morning but she told me I should go. So I did.

The next day, because I felt so guilty for not being there when Mandy was having such a hard time, I called all my vocal students and told them I couldn't give them lessons anymore.

But that only made Mandy madder at me because I'd done it without talking to her about it. No matter how hard I tried, I couldn't win.

I'm not sure what Mandy did when I was at school and at work but when I was in our apartment, she slept most of the time. I wasn't sure if that was because she was tired or because she didn't want to talk to me anymore.

Every time I tried to tell her how sorry I was that I wasn't there when she needed me, she always cut me off, saying, "It wasn't your fault."

She slept during the day but at night she'd sit on our couch and watch TV until late at night and then fall asleep on the couch. So we were never in bed together. I wasn't sure if that was the way it was going to be from now on. But I didn't say anything.

A week later on Saturday morning she waited for me to come back from my custodial job.

"We need to talk," she said.

"Okay." I sat down.

"Not here. On our trail."

"Are you up for that?"

"We don't have to walk. I just want to be there."

We went up the trail for a few steps and then she led me off the trail so we wouldn't be seen by other hikers.

And then we sat down.

"Well here we are again," she said.

"Yes."

She sighed. "Can you believe I thought I'd met my true love just because you could keep up with me on the trail? Talk about shallow, right? I mean, c'mon, what was I thinking?"

I began to wonder if she was going to ask for a divorce.

She continued. "And you were as clueless as I was. You liked me just because I liked the way you sang. We must be the two shallowest people on the earth, right?"

I sighed. "Maybe so."

"I'm curious. Do you ever wish you'd married Hillary instead of me?"

"No. What I wish is that I'd been there with you in the hospital. I shouldn't have waited. I should have got a taxi to drive me to Provo."

"That would've cost a fortune."

"But at least I'd have been there."

She nodded. "That would have been good. Not that it would have made any difference though."

"It would have made a difference."

"In what way?" she asked.

"You wouldn't be mad at me now. You'd talk to me. And you wouldn't pretend to be asleep when I come home after my classes and then watch TV late at night after I've gone to bed."

She sighed. "Our experience the first time we met seems so juvenile now, doesn't it?"

"Juvenile or not, it was the best time I'd ever had with a girl."

She nodded and then sighed. "I don't suppose anyone falling in love ever expects that it's not always going to be the way it is then, that you're going to have disappointments. Nobody ever thinks that."

"That's probably true," I said.

"Remember when I grabbed your cowboy hat and ran away with it, hoping you'd chase me?"

"That was fun."

"Yeah, it was."

She turned to face me. "We're not getting along very well now though, are we? Why do you suppose that is?"

"Because I wasn't with you when you needed me."

She sighed. "That was a huge disappointment to me. I needed you so much, and you weren't there."

I sighed. "I'm so sorry."

"I know you are. But actually there's more to it than that."

"Like what?"

"Well, first of all, it seems to me that you have never grieved the loss of our daughter. That was very hard for me to understand. It made me wonder what you'd do if I died. I figure you'd wait a couple of weeks and then call Hillary and ask her to marry you."

"How can you say that?" I complained.

"Because you haven't shown any grief over the loss of our daughter."

"That's starting to happen. Whenever I see a little girl now, I wonder what it would have been like to have her with us at the age of that girl. And also, if I could have made her laugh, like when I chased her around the house. And if I could have taught her some songs that we could sing together. Things like that." I paused. "I think of her now whenever I see a little girl." I sighed. "Sorry it's taken time for that to happen, but I do miss her now."

She opened up her arms for me. We hugged each other and mourned for the loss of our April.

That helped a little to bridge the gap that had separated us.

We wiped our tears and we held each other again.

She sighed. "For some reason I imagined we'd live a charmed life, and now I know that's not true," she said. "You look like Prince Charming, but you're not. You're just a guy. And I'm just a girl. Neither one of us has any guarantees. I know this shows how immature I am, but having a miscarriage was a big surprise to me." She paused. "Cinderella never had a miscarriage. Goldilocks either. Now I'm afraid of what else might be coming our way."

"Whatever it is, we'll face it and move on."

"That's easier to say than to do," she said.

This was hard for me to say. "Do you want a divorce?"

"No. Do you want to know why? Because no matter who I was married to, I would still have no guarantees that things would be easy. So I might as well stay with you."

"Thank you."

"Don't take any of this personal. I now know that married life can be hard. The only problem is nobody ever knows how hard it's going to be."

"If we can get through this, maybe we'll get through whatever comes our way," I said.

"Maybe so."

"There's something else you should know," she said.

"What?"

"I don't want to get pregnant for at least a couple of years. I can't face the possibility of having another miscarriage again. I hope you will be okay with this."

"Or course."

"You sure?"

"Yeah, I am."

"I was worried about telling you, what with your mom and my dad wanting us to pump out grand-kids for them one right after the other."

"We shouldn't ever do anything just to please them," I said.

"I agree."

"Okay, after dumping on you so much, there's one other thing I need to tell you," she said. "I love you very much."

I sighed. "Thank you for saying that. I love you too. Very much."

She grabbed my cowboy hat. "If I could run, you could chase me and we'd end up kissing."

"We don't actually need to run though, right?"

"Very true. But before that, is there anything you need to tell me?"

"Yeah, there is actually."

"What is it?"

"I got a call today from the Boyer College of Music and Dance in Philadelphia. They'd like to have me come out there for a couple of days.

I'm one of four finalists for two opera scholarships and they want to decide which of us to give the scholarships to."

"Wow! That is good news."

"Yes, but I realize you might not want to move so far east."

"Would it cut down the number of times your mom and my dad would come to see us?"

"I would certainly think so."

"Then I'm all for it."

" Do you want to come out with me to Philadelphia when I go to let them see if they want to give me the scholarship? They wouldn't pay for you, but we could borrow some money for the trip."

"No. I can't travel now. Besides, I'd rather stay here and rest up some more."

"Okay then, I'll call and make arrangements with them."

"Great! Can I borrow your hat? Now that we've discussed the hard things, it's play time, okay? As you will recall, we're very good at that."

I handed her my hat. She walked gingerly for a few seconds, and then stopped, turned around, sat down and said with a big smile, "You'll never catch me now."

I sat down beside her and held her. I was grateful she let me hold her even though I'd messed up by not being with her when she needed me the most, and also because I hadn't mourned our loss with her.

A few minutes later we returned to our apartment. Even the little walking we'd done had exhausted her.

I called Boyer College and arranged to go out to see them in a few days.

CHAPTER SIX

On Wednesday of the next week, I flew to Philly. It wasn't until about nine at night that I landed. I was picked up by a faculty member who dropped me off at a hotel and said he'd be by to pick up me at nine in the morning.

The next morning the four candidates for the two full-ride opera scholarships met together in the dean's office. The schedule was fairly simple. First a tour of the place, then we'd each sing for a group of faculty members, have lunch with them, and then they'd have the four of us do a scene from an opera that none of us were familiar with to see how we'd do. The nods of approval from some of the faculty when I sang caused me to think I'd done okay.

I spent that night in Philly and then flew back the next morning.

Two days after returning to Utah, Boyer College called and offered me a full-ride scholarship until I graduated!

On the second Monday in August, Mandy and I started across country, Mandy's pickup full of our belongings, mostly clothes, bedding, laptops, and kitchen things. (I'd sold my car to a guy in our ward. Poor guy.)

We were on the road for only about ten hours a day. The university had given us the money equivalent of two one-way plane tickets which gave us enough money to stay at some great hotels along the way. We spent at least an hour every morning in their hot tub and pool.

This was the first time we'd ever been able to just relax day after day. It was like a long honeymoon without worrying about how much money we were spending.

We arrived in Philadelphia on Thursday night.

On Friday we found a two bedroom apartment about a mile and a half from Boyer College but just a few hundred feet from a bus stop where I could catch a bus that would get me to the college.

Friday afternoon we moved in. We spent all day Saturday being tourists, visiting many of the historic sites in downtown Philadelphia. For lunch we had Philly cheese steak sandwiches, which we both loved. We also drove out to Valley Forge. We slowly jogged where Washington wintered his army during the Revolutionary War.

"Since you're new to the area, I'd like to tell you some little known facts about George Washington," I said.

She smiled. "Oh, please do!"

"The reason George Washington crossed the Delaware on a row boat is because a few days earlier he'd thrown a silver dollar across the Potomac so he didn't have enough money for train fare."

Mandy laughed. "You are such a wealth of misinformation!"

"Yes, I am. It's a gift really."

She reached for my hand. "One thing about being with you, I'm never bored."

"Me either."

We loved church on Sunday. There were three wards at the meetinghouse located at 39th and Chestnut Street in downtown Philly. On Sunday the building seemed to be the LDS equivalent of the United Nations Building. You had Africans from Liberia. The women wore beautiful, colorful modest dresses. And their husbands wore conservative suits. You had members from the YSA ward, many of them students or young professionals. You had long time Philadelphians of various ethnicities, educations and dialects.

It was exciting for us to be in this mix. In our Sunday School class, you'd have Ph.D.'s answering questions, as well as those who worked hard at jobs that didn't pay much money. But it didn't matter. None of the things which usually divide people divided the members of our ward. Everyone appreciated everyone else. Educational levels didn't matter. Income didn't matter. Speech dialects didn't matter. What people wore to church didn't matter. If a person came to church wearing jeans and a sweatshirt, everyone assumed that was the best he or she had.

One sister, a recent convert, had been called to be the ward chorister. She didn't have a dress so the bishop got her a long skirt she could wear when she was leading the singing. So she'd come in jeans, change into the skirt, lead the singing, go to the rest of her meetings, and then switch back into her street clothes before she left the building. She left the skirt hanging up in the coat rack. She was doing her best to honor the Lord. She was a great example to the rest of us.

After church, on our way to our apartment, Mandy said that one of the members of the ward had told her about the BYU-Idaho Pathway Program. "This is how I can get a college education without putting us in debt. It's an online program and it's very reasonable, about seventy dollars per credit hour."

"Is that all?" I asked. "You want to do it?"

"I'm thinking about it, but first I'll check with BYU and see what they have to offer. But I'll sign up for Pathway today because it's the deadline today. If I change my mind, I'll let them know."

Even after checking with BYU, she still decided to go with Pathway because Pathway groups met once a week and she wanted to get better acquainted with members in Philly.

Monday was my first day at the university. I had two classes in the morning and a singing lesson in the afternoon.

My voice teacher was Professor Klein, a short woman with a German accent. She was never happy about anything I did. Her goal was to teach me how to get more resonance with my voice. And so when I sang, she would say, "Less, less."

Because I couldn't do what she wanted, she was not happy with me.

Day after day all I heard from her was "Less, less."

I had thought I would be practicing arias, but, no, just vocal exercises and "Less, less."

I asked Professor Klein once why we were doing the same exercises over and over again. "It's because you have so many bad habits. You need to learn to focus the vowels more before we do anything else. Less, less."

The reason for saying "Less, less," was because I was forcing everything which made it impossible to achieve optimum resonance. The thing is I didn't know how to sing differently and none of her suggestions made any difference.

I complained so much to Mandy that when she wanted to tease me, she'd say, "Less, less." And then she'd start laughing.

*   *   *

Pathway started the third Thursday in September.

After every Pathway meeting, which they called a gathering, Mandy came home with stories to tell about the discussions they'd had, and the good humored teasing that took place, and the testimonies that had been borne.

She often invited me to come just to see what it was like but I could always come up with a reason not to go.

In mid-October, after weeks of "Less, less," after trying hard to adjust my breathing, my diaphragm, the position of my mouth, for an instant a sound came from me which I had never expected. It was like it was originating a few inches in front of my face, and it was a rich, amazing sound.

"Yes! Yes! Do it again."

At first it wasn't there but then it jumped out again.

"That's it! That's it! Now do it as you go up a scale."

It was not easy, and I would keep slipping out of that sound, but with some concentration, I could get it to come again.

"Do you know what this means?" Professor Klein asked excitedly.

"No, what?"

"It means you could become the next Pavarotti! This was the one thing you were lacking, and now you've achieved it! Congratulations!"

That was the first compliment I'd received from her.

She continued. "The first thing you need to do is to achieve this resonance over your entire range and with every vowel. And the second thing you need to work on is eight different arias as fast as you can."

We picked out the eight arias I would work on. Three of them were from the opera *La Bohéme* by Puccini.

"These must be perfected by December sixth."

"Why by then?"

"I have a friend and colleague who is in charge of hiring new singers for the Metropolitan Opera. We worked together years ago. We share the same birthday, December sixth, and so he will come here then and we will celebrate together. While he's here, I want him to hear you. Hopefully from this will eventually come an offer for you to become full-time with the Metropolitan Opera."

"Are you serious? That would be like a dream come true!" I said.

"Good. We both have a lot of work to do between now and then. So work hard and I'll try to guide you along the way."

I was so excited! The first thing I wanted to do was to tell Mandy but it was Thursday and she'd be at her Pathway gathering, so I decided to go there and be with her and tell her my good news.

Pathway met at the 39th and Chestnut Meetinghouse. When I got there, they were in the middle of their Book of Mormon class. I walked in, grabbed a chair and pulled it up next to her. They had been divided into groups of about six people, sitting at round tables.

She gave me a big hug.

"You know this person?" Sister Johnson, one of the senior missionaries, asked with a big smile on her face.

"Yes, this is my husband David. I invited him to come and see what we do here each week."

"David, it's good to have you with us. Please free to participate in our discussions."

As each group worked to answer the questions they'd been given, I looked around at the people in the class. About a third of them were Hispanic. That group spoke Spanish as they discussed the questions in their groups but they gave their answers to the class in English. There were also five or six that were Black. Not unusual for a ward in Philly, but certainly out of the norm for BYU.

I would have thought Mandy would be a little uncomfortable being there. But she wasn't. I could tell she loved and respected them.

One of the groups was discussing 2nd Nephi Chapter 15, Isaiah Chapter 5. One of the questions had to do with verse 21. "Wo unto the wise in their own eyes and prudent in their own sight."

They were asked to discuss this verse.

One of the Black sisters, whose name was Hannah, said, "Well, what that means is that the Good Lord doesn't have any throw-aways. Take us for instance. Who'd have thought we'd be in college? But look at us! We are! None of us are throw-aways, right? Not a single one." She got a big smile on her face. "Except maybe for our American Indian brother, Brother Comanche, right?"

"I was thinking the same thing about you!" he said.

Everyone laughed.

Mandy told me later that his last name was Camacho but Hannah, as a joke, always pronounced his name wrong and often called him "our Native American brother from Arizona."

There we were, a mixture of races, cultures, backgrounds, and we all felt comfortable with each other. I could see why Mandy loved these people.

On our way home on the bus, I told Mandy about me finally achieving what Professor Klein had been working on with me. By singing a note I showed her the difference. It scared one passenger who moved away from us.

"That does seem much better! Way to go, Davey Boy!"

"She told me I could become the next Pavarotti!"

"Pavarotti the singer or the guy who runs the deli on the corner?" she teased.

"The singer."

"Too bad. I was hoping you could get us a good deal on his potato salad, which is to die for." She started laughing.

"Very funny," I said.

She hugged me. "You, the next Pavarotti? That is great!"

We got off the bus.

"Wait, there's more," I said. "Professor Klein is friends with a guy who hires new talent at the Metropolitan Opera. He's coming December sixth. She wants me to sing for him. This could be our big break!"

"I'm so proud of you!"

Up two flights and we entered our apartment.

"We should celebrate," she whispered in my ear.

I smiled. "I like that idea very much."

"So what do you want to do, go to a movie or play Scrabble?" she teased.

"Got any other choices?"

"Well, just one," she said with a smile.

"I'll take the third choice."

She laughed. "You don't even know what it is."

I smiled "I think I do."

"Okay, that's what we'll do then! How fun! I didn't even know you liked to bowl."

"Are you kidding me? Bowling is my life!"

We had a great time.

*   *   *

Our first calling in our ward was to be Primary choristers. When we were called, our bishop said to us, "The reason we're calling both of you to do this is because the older boys in Primary won't sing because they think that's just for girls. We want you to get them singing, to have them enjoy the experience, and also to teach them the gospel through the songs. You can make a difference in their lives by doing this."

Our first Sunday we played it safe. Mandy had made a poster with the lyrics of the song we were working on that month. It also had cartoon sketches that would help them remember the words.

With the children watching, we put the poster in a closet in the Primary room when we were done with it.

On the next Sunday, when I pulled the poster out of the closet, it had an irregular hole on one of the edges. The hold was about two inches long and an inch wide.

I showed them the poster. "Oh, no! I think our church mouse ate part of our poster during the week. But you can still read it, right? So we'll just go ahead with the song."

Each week there was another hole caused by our church mouse. For some of the children, finding out what that naughty mouse had done was the best part of their day.

Weeks later there were no words, mostly just holes. But by that time, the children already knew the song. And the next week we would start with a new poster which week after week would have more mouse holes in it.

One week the bishop came because his kids had told him about the naughty church mouse. We had him laughing along with all the kids. As he left Primary, he came up and shook our hands and told us he very much appreciated our efforts with these kids.

One Sunday while Mandy was leading the kids in a song, I showed up in a costume I'd borrowed from the college. I was dressed as a traffic cop.

"Pardon me, Ma'am, but I'd like to try to lead the children in a song," I said.

"Do you even know how to lead singing?"

"Oh, yes, ma'am."

"Well, okay, maybe one song won't do any harm."

I did it like a traffic cop. When I wanted some of the kids not to sing, I blew my police whistle and put my hand out like I was stopping traffic. When I wanted them all to sing, I waved them on.

A member of the bishopric was in with us but he wasn't singing. By prior arrangement with him over the phone earlier that week, I went up to him and blew my whistle.

"I'm going to have to give you a ticket, sir."

"What for?"

"Failure to sing. That's a pretty serious charge, let me tell you."

I started to write him out a ticket.

"Please give me another chance!" he pleaded.

"Well, okay, I'll give you one more chance. Stand up here with me so the children can hear you sing."

He started singing, but by my previous arrangement, he sounded awful.

I stopped everyone.

"What do you think I should do here?" I asked the kids.

"Make him stop!" one of the older boys called out.

"Sir, I've changed my mind. If the kids here can do a better job singing our song, I'm going to let you off the hook and request that if you ever visit us again, please don't sing."

The kids stood up and sang it again and they'd never sounded better.

Every week we tried to make it fun for them and for us.

But we did something else. With each song, the first time we did it, we tried to explain, in simple terms, whatever doctrine that the song dealt with.

I even got the boys to sing out too. I had them stand up in front of everyone. First I taught them how to breathe and then I taught them how to stand. And then I showed them how to put their right hand out and belt out a note like they were in an opera.

They loved it! The only trouble is that they started singing every song that way, standing up with great posture and the one-handed "I'm an opera singer" stance.

What a great calling it was for the two of us to be Primary choristers. We were having so much fun!

    *   *   *

In the days leading up to December sixth, I had never worked so hard as I tried to master eight arias and master the vocal techniques Professor Klein had taught me.

In our apartment at night I drove Mandy crazy, standing in front of our bathroom mirror, singing one note at a time, trying to achieve what Professor Klein had taught me. She often went shopping just to get away from that.

In my daily time with Professor Klein, she had us listen to Pavarotti recordings. She pointed out good things he was doing, and I tried to practice it and then took notes so I'd be able to reproduce it again.

Every Thursday morning Mandy asked if I'd be able to attend Pathway with her that night. I usually said no because I felt under such pressure to do well on December sixth.

On December sixth, I went to Professor Klein's office at 2 pm and met Vladimir Pyrenko. He was a large rotund man with a mustache and a ring of hair around the edges but not much on top. He grabbed my hand and shook it with great enthusiasm. "So this is the young genius Sadie is always talking about! It's a pleasure to meet you!"

"As it is for me!" I exclaimed.

Professor Klein handed him a list of the eight arias I was prepared to sing for him.

"Ah, yes, these are good. Let's start with this one."

With Professor Klein accompanying me, I sang three arias. After each one he nodded his head. "Very good."

He had picked two songs from *La Bohéme*. He told us that he'd picked them because the Met was going to do that opera soon and he wanted to compare my singing with one of their premiere tenors.

"Very nice indeed!" he said after I finished my next aria. He shook my hand. "When Professor Klein is through with you, give me a call and we'll make arrangements for you to come up and try out. I wouldn't be surprised if you were offered a contract to come work for us."

When I left Professor Klein's office, I was so excited. I called Mandy.

"Vladimir loves my singing!"

"Oh my gosh, Davey Boy! That is so great! Congratulations! You did it! I'm so proud of you!"

"I'll tell you all about it when I get home!"

"I'm going to the deli and get something for us to have to celebrate!"

"Great! I'm on my way!"

On my way home, I thought, *what would I do without Mandy? She makes success more of a big deal. Without her, I'd have nobody to cheer me on. Except my mom. But she'd tell me to come to San Francisco where she and Mandy's dad had decided to stay each winter. And that would be more for her benefit than my career.*

*   *   *

Early In the morning of the second Thursday in January, I got a call from Professor Klein. "Vladimir just called. The lead tenor and his backup went out for lunch together yesterday and they've both come down with food poisoning. Neither one of them will be able to sing tonight and maybe not tomorrow night either. Vladimir wants to know if you could play the part of Rodolfo tonight and possibly tomorrow night. I remember you telling me you played Rodolfo at BYU. Do you remember it enough to do it tonight?"

"Yes, of course. I listen to it every day on my way to school."

"All right then. I'll tell him. Vladimir will charter a plane to fly you to LaGuardia this morning. Pack up a few things and get out to the airport there in Philly and I'll call when I have more details nailed down."

Mandy was still in bed. She had stayed up late to do her homework assignment for Pathway.

"Mandy, guess what! I have good news! I'm leaving for NYC. The Met has two of its tenors sick with the flu. I'm going to fill in tonight as Rodolfo in *La Bohéme* at the Met!"

She came to me, held my face in her hands and kissed me. "How wonderful! What do you need me to do?"

"I don't know. I'll just start throwing things into my bag. Could you make me an egg sandwich?"

"Yes, of course."

As she cooked, she'd call out things like, "Got your toothpaste?"

And I'd answer, "Yeah, I got that."

She started laughing. "You got your Yankee pajamas? They'll fit right in there."

I'd actually retired my Yankee pajamas because every time I wore them, Mandy made fun of me.

"How about an umbrella? It rains a lot in NYC."

"Good idea."

"You think I should take mass transit or get a cab to the Philly Airport or drive?" I asked.

"A cab. They'll reimburse you for your out- of-pocket expenses."

"Okay." I called for a cab.

We stood at the window where we could see the cab when it pulled up.

"You haven't told me you wished I was going with you."

"You want to go with me? That'd be great."

"Actually, I don't want to go with you. What I want is for you to tell me you wished I would go with you."

"I do. Very much!"

A cab pulled up in front of our apartment building.

"Okay, the cab's here. Wish me luck!"

"How about we pray before you go?" she asked.

"What about the cab?"

"Go tell him you got to pray with your wife before you go."

I looked at her to see if she was kidding or not. She wasn't. "Okay. I'll be right back."

I ran down the stairs and told the cab driver I'd be a few minutes more. He nodded.

I ran back up the stairs.

"Let's have a kneeling prayer," she said.

I looked at her like she was crazy, but knelt down beside her.

"I'm too nervous to pray," I gasped. "Would you pray for us?"

We knelt down and prayed. What I remember about her prayer was her saying, "And please bless Davey to have Thy help when he sings that he may feel Thy love and Thy support for him. Bless him also to use his talents to bless others, especially those that some people might overlook and think aren't important. In the name of Jesus Christ. Amen."

We got up and hugged. "I love you so much," I said. "Thank you for your prayer. That's exactly what I needed."

"Go sing, make family proud!" she said with an oriental accent.

We hugged and kissed and then I hurried down the stairs.

By the time I was on ground level, she yelled out from an open window, "I love you!"

"I love you too! Thanks for everything."

*   *   *

Once I reached NYC, following the instructions Vladimir gave me on my phone, I took a cab to the New York Hilton where they had booked a room for me. I checked in and then got another cab to the Met.

Everything about the experience was intimidating, the other singers, the stage, the set, the costumes I was to wear. The whole atmosphere of the place made me feel like a hopeless outsider.

"So what is this, amateur night? I can't believe they got you," the soprano playing Mimi said right before we practiced a duet together. "Ten thousand tenors in this town and Vladimir picks some clown from Philly. Go figure. Try not to make me look bad, okay?"

After we sang, she said, "You know what? You did that quite well."

"Thanks. And let me say how much of an honor it is for me to have the opportunity to sing with you."

She nodded like she was thinking, *Of course it is*.

Unfortunately this was not just about singing. It was knowing where on stage I needed to be, when I needed to be there, and when and where to exit, and even who was playing which part. And I had to interact with others as if we were old friends, but we were strangers, and, actually, they were also not happy that the replacement for Rodolfo was not one of their friends.

Every time I panicked, I remembered Mandy's prayer and it helped me be calmer.

Vladimir told me he'd be with me offstage, giving me directions and tips that would help me get through the night.

"You can do this," he said. "And if you pull this off tonight, your future success is guaranteed. Just keep saying to yourself, *'I can do this.'* And the truth is you can do this. I'm sure of that. That's why I asked you."

Just before I was to go on, I remember looking out at the huge audience and being totally intimidated by what I was about to do. But then as I remembered Mandy's prayer about being there for those whom others might overlook, I spotted a man in the audience. He was wearing a tie and an old gray sweater. He had his daughter with him, a girl maybe in the sixth grade. She wore glasses and had on a pink dress. I could tell by the way she kept looking around and pointing out things to her dad that she was delighted to be there. Her dad was dressed in clothes that made me think that he was not rich and that this was done with some sacrifice for this daughter that he loved so much. And that this might be the only opera he and his daughter would ever attend together at the Met.

Because of this dad's sacrifice for his daughter, I decided to ignore all the wealthy folks in the big-money seats and focus my performance on this one dad and his daughter.

This is for you guys, I thought.

And then it was my time to go on, and I did. And I felt peace of mind.

Three hours later it was over.

We got a standing ovation.

And then they announced that I had filled in at the last moment and flown in from Boyer College in Philadelphia that very day. They gave me a huge standing ovation.

Even the little girl and her dad stood up and clapped. When I made eye contact with them, I pointed to them and then threw them a kiss. They were both surprised I'd noticed them. I had Mandy to thank for that.

An hour later I returned to my hotel room. I was exhausted but I knew Mandy would be waiting for me to call.

"Hi," I said.

"I'm so glad you called. How did it go?"

"Great! I got a standing ovation!"

"Wow! That is so great! I'm so happy for you."

"Your prayer helped a great deal."

"In what way?"

I told her about focusing my attention on the dad and his daughter.

"Thank you for telling me that."

"I'm exhausted now. I just wanted you to know how it went. I'll tell you all about it when I get home. I'm not sure if they'll need me tomorrow or not, but I'll let you know. Vladimir said he'd call me in the morning."

"Okay. I can't wait for you to get back."

"Well, okay, goodnight. I love you."

"I love you too! Thanks for calling. Good night."

They didn't need me for the performance the next day so I flew back to Philly.

A few days later Vladimir sent me newspaper clippings from several New York papers, extolling my performance on such a short notice. This is what he wrote in his short note. "I can say with some confidence that your future success is assured. Congratulations on a job well done!"

I was now on the path that had been my lifelong dream.

CHAPTER SEVEN

As word of my successful debut at the Met spread, I suddenly had many opportunities to perform for a wide variety of audiences, including a banquet attended by the mayor of Philadelphia, the governor of Pennsylvania, and many other dignitaries.

About this time Mandy started substituting as a physical education teacher. She worked one or two times a week. Some of the schools were quite good. Others had discipline problems. A P.E. teacher handles that by having the trouble makers run laps for the whole period. If they didn't run fast enough, she'd run with them and embarrass them for not keeping up.

One of the projects Professor Klein and I began working on was to release a CD featuring the arias I had worked on in preparation for Vladimir's first visit. The proceeds would benefit the college's music scholarship fund. Instead of just a piano we needed to arrange music for several instruments. In addition we needed to work with the alumni association on marketing.

Every Thursday Mandy asked me to come with her to Pathway on Thursday night. I was always too busy.

After Pathway each week, she always had stories to tell.

One Friday morning while we were eating breakfast, she said, "Something I found out last night. You remember Hannah, right? She has a great sense of humor and she's always pronouncing Brother Camacho's name wrong. Well, last night I found out that she comes early every week to set up chairs and roll the round tables into our room so Elder and Sister Johnson won't have to. Every week! Who gives service like that?"

"Nobody I've ever known."

"I know. Me either. Oh, and Sister Rodrigues. She was the one who was pregnant. Well, last week she had her baby and this week she was at Pathway with her baby!"

"Wow!"

"That shows how much Pathway means to her."

"I guess so."

"One of the Hispanic sisters told me last week, 'This is our only hope.' Think of what this program can provide for them. They can get better jobs if they are, first of all, comfortable with speaking English, and, two, if they have a technical certificate, or an associate degree, or a bachelor's degree."

"Yeah, it's a great program."

"Oh, there's one other thing. I don't know if you remember Claudia or not. She's older than the others in the class. She's an amazing cook and every week she brings the most delicious desserts to share. She often gives me some to take to you."

"How come I've never seen any of these desserts?" I asked.

Long pause. "Well, of course, it's a very long bus ride back to our apartment."

I started laughing. "You're eating the dessert she's asked you to give to me?"

"Next time I'll ask her to give me two extra desserts, one for me on my way home and one for you. You will like them so much."

"I'm sure I will, if I ever see them."

"I'll work on that. Oh, one more story from Pathway. Sister Lopez works in a convenience store. She works six days a week, ten hours a day. Tonight she told me that a couple of days ago her boss told her she was lazy because she didn't work on Sundays. Sister Lopez told him she couldn't do that because she had to go to church with her family every Sunday. Her boss goes, 'Well maybe I'll get someone else to take your place.' So that was really worrying Sister Lopez."

Mandy continued. "I told her, 'Look at you, Sister. You're taking an online college course. You're leading discussions in English. You're earning college credit. You're way too qualified for the job you have. You won't have any trouble at all getting another job that will pay you more money!' After I told her that, she got a big smile on her face because she knew that what I'd told her is true."

"Good for you for telling her that."

"And the thing is, it is true. Just the fact she's speaking English will qualify her for a better job. Also, I'm sure her boss was just trying to threaten her. But it didn't work."

"Great story," I said.

After a long pause, Mandy said, "Why don't you care about these people as much as I do?"

"Because you spend more time with them."

"I hope that's it." She sighed. "I'm a little afraid that with all your recent success you're going to end up somebody who only cares about himself."

"Why would you think that?"

"You ought to listen to yourself lately. It's always my successful debut at the Met, my prodigious talent, my loyal fans, my first CD, my promising future."

"I'm doing it for you too."

"Even if that's true, it's not enough."

"What do you mean it's not enough?"

"Be careful, Davey. Don't go around thinking you're better than anyone else just because you can sing some obscure song that most people don't care about anyway."

I looked at my watch. "I need to go."

"Not yet. Remember this. I love you more than anyone else in the world. You're the first thing I think of when I wake up and the last thing I think of when I go to sleep. I will always love you. But I do worry that sometime I might not respect you. That's why I'm talking to you about this."

"What do you want me to do?"

"I want you to think about the people you usually ignore, the ones you overlook, the ones you don't care about, the ones who aren't good singers, who will never have a college degree, the ones who are doing the best they can with the hand they've been dealt. Do you ever pay any attention to the people you pass on the street? Do you ever wonder about their lives? About their challenges?"

"Not really," I said.

"Okay, me either actually, or at least I didn't until just recently. But then I came to love the members of my Pathway group. I love them so much. I feel so good being with them. I want you to feel that way about the people you meet every day. They're all children of God. And even if you don't know or care about their lives, Father in Heaven does."

She grabbed a notebook she used for Pathway and thumbed through it until she found a page, ripped it out and gave it to me. "These are lyrics to a song I have been trying to write. I'd like you to come up with a melody to go with it. It's based on something Hannah said one day in one of our discussions. She said, 'God doesn't have any throwaways.' So here's my lyrics." She began to read the lyrics to me.

My Lord He has no throwaways,
There's no one He don't love.
All the folks you see today.
Are loved by Him above.

I nodded. "Good job," I said.

"Okay, this is the second verse, but it needs some work," she said.

He loves his children, every one
And we should love them too.
It doesn't matter where they live
They came from Heaven too.

"It's got a real good message," I said.

"I know the lyrics need some work, and I'll keep working on that, but could you make up a melody for it?" she asked. "Or are you too busy for that too?" she asked.

"Of course not. I'll do it today."

"That'd be great!"

I didn't have any chance to work on Mandy's song during the day but Professor Klein wanted to critique my first version CD of my songs after she'd finished with some private lessons which would be at eight that night. So while I waited for her, I went to a practice room and knocked out a melody for the song. I spent about an hour on it, and by the time I finished, it seemed to fit the lyrics.

It wasn't until nine thirty that I was finished with Professor Klein.

I'd just left the building humming Mandy's song, heading to a bus stop.

And that is when I got held up at gunpoint and remembered the lyrics Mandy had come up with. So in trying to find why this guy was not a throw-away, I asked him if he could sing.

Once we got over him threatening to shoot me, we started to make some progress. "Okay, I'm going to start singing a song I know. It's called *Amazing Grace*. And then you sing it an octave lower."

"What that mean?"

"Okay, I'll sing this." I did a few measurers of the song. "Now you sing it lower like this. "Amazing. Okay, do it."

After a couple of tries we had it.

"Very good! You have a great voice and can carry a tune."

"Carry it where?"

"That means you can sing. Let's go stand over by where the buses come. We'll see if we can make some money singing. Whatever we get you can have. Okay?"

He shook his head. "If cop come, you say take me jail."

"Okay, look, give me back my ten dollars, and then it will be like you didn't rob me so I can't have you arrested. Right?"

He handed me back my money.

We sang for about half an hour. In that time, we had several people give us some money. It was a little over fifteen dollars.

I handed the money to him. "You are now a professional singer! Look at the money you made!"

"I like this much!"

"Come to my office sometime and I can help you be a better singer. Then I might be able to get you a steady job singing opera."

"Why you do this for me?"

"Your voice has some good qualities. With a lot of work, I think you could make it big time."

"Big time?"

"Look, a good opera singer can make, like, 1000 dollars a week." I wrote the number on a scrap piece of paper from my coat pocket.

His mouth dropped open. "Much good!"

"I know. So come and I'll teach you. See that building over there? That's where folks like you become opera singers. Could you meet me there like tomorrow in the afternoon? My office is room 320." I wrote on the paper I'd just given him. "If you could come anytime between five and six o'clock, I'll be there. It will take about an hour."

"Bring wife?"

"Yes, you can bring your wife."

"She speak English good." He paused. "And bring baby girl?"

"Yes, of course."

"I come. Thank you for help me!" We shook hands and then he left.

When I got to our apartment, Mandy asked me how my day had gone. So I told her.

"You asked a guy robbing you at gunpoint if he could sing? You don't ask robbers that!"

"Why not?"

"He could have shot you just for asking that! I certainly would've."

"Well, I knew he had a good voice. Not all robbers do, you know."

"So he's coming to your office for a singing lesson? Will you have him arrested?"

"No. I talked him into giving me the money back. So that means he didn't rob me. So there's no reason for me to call the cops on him."

"So basically your newest best friend in Philly is a robber, right?"

"Retired robber. Oh, also, he's bringing his wife and their daughter."

"Why is he doing that?"

"He told me his wife speaks English good."

"Well," she said, correcting me.

"And also maybe so she'll be proud of him. Like you're proud of me sometimes."

"Not now of course," she said with a smile.

"Can you speak Spanish?" I asked. "I mean, besides taco, tortilla, and fried beans."

She laughed. "You actually think fried beans is Spanish, don't you?"

"Yes, of course. Everybody knows that."

She laughed. "Well, okay, I did take Spanish for two years in high school. And I have been practicing a little with my Pathway friends."

"What would you think about being with me when they come?" I asked.

"Are you crazy? Absolutely not!"

"How come?"

"Because we don't know them."

"What's all this talk from you about My Lord, He has no throwaways?"

"Oh, sure, throw that in my face!"

"You can talk to his wife while I'm working with him on his singing."

"What are their names?"

"He didn't give me his name. Robbers are funny that way."

She started laughing. "Why is it that every time anything significant happens in your life, you go away from it not knowing the person's name?"

"I knew your first name, okay? So it could have been worse."

She scowled at me. "Yeah, I suppose. But how about your robber friend's name?"

"Actually the police discourage asking a guy who's robbing you at gunpoint what his name is."

She sighed. "Okay, I'll come meet them. But I will have the cops on speed dial."

And so the next day, a little before five, Mandy and I were in Room 320 waiting for what Mandy called my robber friend.

"Don't say anything awkward to them when they show up," Mandy suggested.

"Like what?"

"You're late. What held you up?" she said.

We started laughing. "Or I'd like you to meet my wife. She's a cop," I said.

We kept coming up with things like that so by the time there was a knock on the door, we opened the door with big smiles on our faces.

"Come in, come in!" I said. They walked in looking very nervous.

"My name is David," I said, shaking my robber friend's hand. "And this is my wife Mandy."

He turned to his wife who spoke for both of them. "I am Maria and my husband's name is Alejandro. And this is our daughter Angelina."

"Oh, look at her! She is so beautiful!" Mandy exclaimed about Angelina.

"Thank you. We brought you some guacamole," Maria said, handing Mandy a small container.

"Oh, thank you! We will all enjoy it together later tonight."

"Well, let's get to work," I said to Alejandro. "First thing we'll do is some exercises."

A minute later Mandy, Maria and their daughter were bored. "I'll show them around the place," Mandy said.

Twenty minutes later I began to work with Alejandro on a baritone solo from "La Traviata" by Verdi.

Hearing Alejandro sing brought Mandy and Maria and Angelina back into the practice room. But now Angelina was in Mandy's arms.

"Your daddy is singing good, isn't he?" Mandy asked.

She smiled. "Daddy!"

And a short time later we were done. "Very good!" I said, shaking Alejandro's hand. "Can you come back next week at the same time?"

"Yes, thank you!"

"Can you practice during the week?" I asked.

They both shook their heads. "We are living with my parents and they don't like noise," Maria said.

"They could come to the church on Thursday during Pathway," Mandy said. "There are lots of rooms he could practice in."

And so that's what we arranged.

On Thursday night, Alejandro, Maria and Angelina came to the 39th and Chestnut meeting house. We had them come at 6 pm so Mandy could say hello to Angelina and fuss over her before Pathway started at six thirty.

It worked great. Alejandro, Maria, Angelina and I used the Young Women's room on the opposite side of the building from where the Pathway group met.

About an hour later, Mandy had a break and came and joined us. Angelina, seeing her, ran and threw her arms around her.

"Oh, you sweet child!" Mandy exclaimed.

"What are the other people here for?" Maria asked.

"It's called Pathway. It's a way for people to get a college education."

"College? That costs so much," Maria said.

"It costs only about fifteen dollars a week."

She looked confused.

"Would you like to sit in on our class tonight?" Mandy asked.

She looked worried.

"You won't have to say anything."

After a few seconds, she nodded her head. So Mandy left with Maria and Angelina to go to Pathway.

Half an hour later Alejandro and I joined them. We sat with our wives and Angelina at a large round table that had ten Hispanics in Pathway. They seemed very happy to have these newcomers with them.

I'm not sure what they said to him during the class discussion but he kept nodding his head as he learned more about Pathway.

After the Pathway gathering, we walked with them to the subway stop. "We want to be in Pathway," Maria said. "What we have to do?"

"Well, first you need to become a member of our Church," I said.

"How do we do that?"

"Well, we have some young men and young women here. They are called missionaries. They can meet with you both and explain the teachings of our church."

And so the missionaries began to teach Alejandro and Maria, twice a week in our apartment. We loved being with them and seeing them make progress as they read and prayed and attended church. For me it was like being a missionary except I liked my companion much better. Also, Mandy loved being with Angelina. She took care of her during each lesson.

Four weeks later Alejandro and Maria asked me to baptize them.

I was honored to do that for them.

* * *

A week later, when Alejandro came for a singing lesson, he brought two others with him. One was his cousin, a woman about the same age as Alejandro. The second visitor was a neighbor in her early twenties.

"We want to sing in a group," Maria said. "Practice each week. Sing for fun and for money."

"You need more than you guys to sing in a group."

"We have thirty. We want to sing opera," Alejandro said.

"Why?"

"Rich people give us money if we sing opera."

Tell them no, I thought. *I have more important things to do than this. I need to press ahead with my goal of being hired full time at the Met and then later singing in the great opera theaters of the world, to be known and respected throughout the world. Leading a bunch of illegal alien amateurs doing opera badly is not my dream. I'm so much better than that.*

But then Mandy's accursed lyrics came into my mind.

My Lord He has no throwaways,
There's no one He don't love.
All the folks you see today
Are loved by Him above.

And so, against my better judgement, I told them I'd work with them and we'd see how it went.

When we met a week later, there were over forty people there.

"This is more people than you told me were coming," I told Alejandro.

"I sang for them and they all said they wanted to learn to sing too," he said.

"Okay, look if any of them can't sing, we can't keep them. I need to listen to each one."

After listening to them all, I had Alejandro tell five of them we couldn't have them in the choir but we'd like them to help out in other ways.

So now we had a choir.

What I eventually learned from all this is that sometimes we use the term illegal aliens as an excuse not to treat people as our equals. It's like, "Well if these are illegal aliens, I certainly don't want to have anything to do with them." We do the same with people who can't speak English.

It's a convenient excuse for us to maintain our distance. But the thing is, if you spend time with them, you come to love them. And that's what happened to Mandy and me with the people in this singing group.

Mandy attended our practices so she could translate what I said to the singers. Once in a while, though, I'd try to talk to them in Spanish, which caused them all to start laughing, and that was okay with me. We were all learning. They were learning to sing and speak English, and they were seeing me struggle with Spanish.

They worked very hard for me at our practices. But what was even more impressive, they practiced every day in their apartments during the week.

Also, they brought food with them that we could all enjoy during our breaks. I especially liked the homemade guacamole.

One time when I was ranting about them making the same mistake over and over, Mandy stood up and announced, "Quick, somebody, guacamole!"

Maria ran to where the food was and put some guacamole on a tortilla chip and ran over to me like she was about to administer first aid. I opened my mouth and she put the tortilla chip into my mouth. I got a big smile on my face. And everyone started laughing.

"Life is good!" I shouted as if demonstrating the difference in me when I had guacamole in my life and when I did not.

Mandy leaned over and whispered. "In Spanish it's 'La vida es buena.'"

I shouted that out and got a standing ovation.

We all were laughing.

"How do I say I love them?" I asked Mandy.

"Te quiero," she said.

I shouted that out and got a second standing ovation. It was a great day for us all. Life was good.

The only possible problem with all this is that we were such a big group we were doing this in a classroom at the university without having cleared anything. As our choir grew to fifty people, I started to worry what would happen when this came to the knowledge of the administration.

"You need to tell them," Mandy would often say.

"I will."

"When?"

"Sometime."

Sometime came one Saturday when our choir sang at a choir member's town celebration. The only problem was that when we were introduced, the governor of the state was there because he had grown up in that neighborhood. And the person introducing us mentioned that we were an opera group sponsored by Boyer College. After we sang, the governor stepped up to the microphone and said he was so pleased that people of all ethnic origins could and should appreciate the great music of the ages.

Of course that was newsworthy and was covered by the media.

The next morning I had a message on my phone in my office saying that the university president needed to talk to me immediately. I hurried to his office.

"What have you been doing here behind my back?" he raged.

I told him the story.

"Why didn't you come to me and tell me about this? The governor called this morning and congratulated me on my leadership in developing this program. I thanked him for his interest. He asked if we needed more funding. I said I'd have to get back to him on that."

He pointed his finger at me. "Don't you ever leave me in the dark again on something you're doing that affects this college! You got that?"

"Yes sir. I would have told you but it sort of snowballed and I wasn't sure if you'd even approve."

He stood up. "Do you have any idea what you've done?" he asked.

I feared the worst. I sighed. "No sir."

"You've shown that opera has a place in all cultures, in all economic levels, and for all people. I've been trying to do that for twenty years and you do it in a few months? Congratulations!" He came over to me and shook my hand.

"Thank you, sir."

"Keep up the good work but keep me informed! From now on you can have a budget of five thousand dollars a year for whatever you need to keep this going. If you need more, let me know."

Over the next few days, I did several TV, newspaper and magazine interviews. In one of the interviews, I told about how it got started, by me getting held up at gunpoint by a man with an exceptional voice.

A few days later the mayor phoned our university president and proposed a plan to encourage neighborhoods in Philly to celebrate a day of music. He suggested they call it "Rob an Opera Guy Day." In later discussions, because they didn't want to be seen as encouraging armed robbery, they revised it to "Stop an Opera Guy" which finally ended up as "Stop an Op" Day.

It was after they'd set it up that they asked me to be a part of this celebration.

Basically my assignment each time was to show up in an elaborate opera costume, enter singing an opera aria and then have somebody pretend to rob me. And then I would call out, "Can anybody here sing?" And then the festivities would begin.

On our first "Stop an Op" Day, there were six communities in Philly that took part.

Of course not all the music came from operas. However, the reason why it was advantageous to have some opera music was because it brought in people with money who loved opera. They spent their money on food, jewelry, and clothes. So in that sense opera was now seen as a great unifier.

News about the event went viral which gave the choir and me a great deal of publicity. Within two weeks, I'd had three offers to join an opera company, the first from Phoenix, another from San Diego, and the third from San Francisco, my home town.

My mom desperately wanted us to move to San Francisco. Mandy's dad said he didn't care if we moved or not as long as I had a job.

Mandy and I had a decision to make, to stay where we were or to move. Which led her to say one Saturday morning, "We need to take a hike."

We decided to go to Valley Forge Park where there were lots of places to walk. We'd grown so used to using mass transit in Philly that just being on the road again in Mandy's pickup made it seem like a vacation.

It was early March so there were still patches of snow on the ground but we could always find a trail where we could avoid walking through the snow.

Once there, we walked for about fifteen minutes before Mandy got serious. "Okay, tell me what your thoughts are about whether we should move or stay in Philly," she said.

"The only place I really want is to be associated with is the Met."
"What about your choir here?" she asked.
"If we leave here, the college will get someone else to lead them."
"But they love you so much. And you love them too, right?"
I sighed. "Yeah, I do love them."

"The times I've been the most proud of you are seeing you work with them. Your patience, you making everything fun for them, your pride when they get what you're trying to explain. It makes me fall in love with you all over again. You give them opportunities they've never had before, and that shows them they can accomplish any goal. It shows them they can compete with anyone in any arena. That's a great lesson for them to have learned."

"Thanks, but what you do with them is equally valid. They learn from you that even though this is serious business, they can still have fun doing it."

"How do I do that?" she asked.

I laughed. "By making fun of me once in a while. They love you for that."

"What they love is that I can make you laugh, which makes you be less scary for them."

"Yeah, that's probably true," I said.

"We're actually a good combination," she said.

"We are. What do you worry about if I take another job?"

"That you'll quit serving others and just concentrate on your career."

I sighed. "I suppose that could happen."

She touched my arm. "I've spent so much time watching you look in the mirror at yourself. I know you're working on vocal techniques when you do that but it does make me think of you sometimes as egotistical and self-absorbed. I grew up with a dad who never paid much attention to himself. So seeing you spend hours looking in the mirror at yourself while you sing is always a little offsetting for me."

"Okay," I said.

"But here's the good news. When you're with your choir, you're focusing on them. You show them great respect. You're okay with me teasing you in front of them. That's a good look for you."

"Thanks."

"So the question for me is if you end up a big star at the Met, will there be more focusing on yourself and less trying to help others?"

"Good question."

"Sorry to rain on your parade."

"No, it's good we're talking about this".

She put her hand on my arm. "Look, bottom line. I'll go where you want to go, but I'd appreciate if you'd at least pray about this decision."

"I will. I promise."

She cleared her throat. "Oh, I should probably mention one other thing. If possible, I'd like my baby to be born here in Philly where all my friends are."

"Baby? What baby? You said you didn't want to have a baby for a couple of years," I said.

"I know but spending time with Alejandro and Maria's little Angelina changed my mind. I decided I want one of those for us. In fact that's the main reason we're taking this walk. I'm expecting a baby. I just found out this morning when my doctor's office called. My due date is in November."

I threw my arms around her. "That's great! Do you know yet what it will be?"

"I'm pretty sure it will either be a boy or a girl."

"You know what? I'd be happy with either of those. Since we're here at Valley Forge, I think we should choose a name that honors George Washington."

"We're not calling him George or Washington. Besides, what would you call it if it's a girl?"

"We could call her Georgy Girl," I teased.

We both started laughing.

Mandy, still laughing, added, "Or we could call her "My first name is Georgy and my middle name is Yes My Dad Is Crazy."

"That's a very long middle name."

"No problem. We can shorten the middle name to "Dad's Crazy."

"See I knew we could reach a compromise."

She reached for my hand. "You do know that I love you and that I'm very proud of you, right?"

"Yeah, I do. And I'm grateful for that."

"Okay, Davey, chase me up the hill. Show me what you got."

"You're pregnant."

"So what? I can still beat you up the hill."

"I seriously doubt that."

We did a halfhearted chase until I caught up with her and we kissed.

"Just like old times," I said.

"This never gets old, does it?" she asked

"Nope, never."

"Have I told you lately that I love you way more than I did when we first got married?" she asked.

"I don't think so."

"Well, I do. Much more," she said.

"Thank you. I feel the same way about you. Also, thank you for telling me when I'm on the wrong track."

She smiled. "I'm always happy to do that. And to tell you when I think you're amazing, which is most of the time."

"Okay, let's compromise," I said. "How about if we stay here in Philly at least until you've had your baby?"

And so we agreed to stay in Philly for at least another year.

That was a little hard for me. I was afraid the Met would forget about me and I'd never have another chance to work there full time.

But the best news was that Mandy was going to have a baby!

CHAPTER EIGHT

Mandy's due date was mid-November, but once Mandy told her dad and my mom that she was pregnant, they wanted to come visit us. They decided to come over the Fourth of July.

That was fine, except we told them my choir was going to perform three times at the Freedom Square on the Fourth. They said that was no problem and that they'd very much like to be there for it.

They booked a hotel near there so we wouldn't have to drive them around.

We first sang at eleven o'clock to a very enthusiastic audience.

We'd catered a lunch for everyone in the choir, using funds provided by the university. We invited our folks to eat with us.

"I couldn't help but notice that you have mostly Mexicans in the choir," my mom said.

"No, that's not true. We have some from Guatemala, Nicaragua, Brazil, Chile, and the Dominican Republic."

"Couldn't you get better singers if you had some whites too?" she asked.

"Not really."

"And you got Blacks too," my mom said.

"Yes we do."

"I just don't see why you're wasting your time with these people," my mom said.

That made me mad but I didn't want to start an argument. "Careful, Mom. These are our best friends," I replied.

"Tell them how this choir started," Mandy said with a big grin on her face.

"Oh, I don't want to bore them with that," I said.

"Okay, I will. Well, it turns out that one night Davey was robbed at gunpoint." My mom always cringed when Mandy called me Davey.

Mandy continued, "When he noticed that the robber had a really good deep bass voice, so he asked him if he could sing. Eventually he talked the guy into coming and taking voice lessons. That's him over there. He was the one who sang 'Old Man River' today. Great voice, right?"

"He tried to rob you? Why didn't you call the police and have him arrested?" my mom asked me.

"Because I talked him into giving me back the money so he'd be in the clear. So after he did that, he hadn't committed a crime."

"And what about everyone else in the choir?" my mom asked. "Are they also robbers, thieves, and drug dealers?"

"We've never asked them what they do for a living. The reason they're in the choir is because they can sing," Mandy said.

Mandy's dad shook his head. "Do you ever feel like you're wasting your time with these people?"

"No. Not ever. This has been the most rewarding experience we've had here in Philly," I said. I turned to Mandy. "Tell them about your song."

She sang her song "No Throwaways Here."

"Yeah, that's real good," her dad said.

"Davey wrote the melody. It's good, right?" Mandy said, turning to my mom.

"Yes, of course," my mom said, like it was an unpleasant duty she had to perform. She sighed. "At least you're pregnant. I was worried that if you couldn't have any children of your own, you'd end up adopting some Black or Hispanic baby."

"Why would you object to that?" Mandy asked.

"I'm not sure I could relate to a grandchild like that," my mom said.

"Blacks and Hispanics are just like any other people except for one thing," Mandy said.

"What's that?" my mom asked.

Mandy smiled. "They don't waste a lot of money going to tanning booths."

My mom frowned. "You don't need to be so cavalier about this."

"Then change the subject," Mandy said.

"Are you planning on raising your child in this environment?" my mom asked.

"Either here or in New York City," Mandy said.

"Either of those cities is no place to raise a child."

I laughed. "Oh, and San Francisco is better? I don't think so."

My mom's eyes started to tear up. "This is not what I had thought would happen. And it's happening to all my friends. Things are not turning out the way we had thought with our children." She sighed. "But life goes on."

"Yeah, it does, Mom," I said. "And at least you can take comfort from the fact that Mandy and I are very happy here."

She took a deep breath. "Yes, of course, you're right. That's what's most important. It's just that I had always pictured my grandchildren living close to my house and walking over for homemade cookies after school. I can see now that's not going to happen. But I'll adjust to this. It will just take a little time, that's all."

"What about you, Dad?" Mandy asked.

He nodded. "I always pictured myself teaching my grandchildren how to ride a horse, and taking them into the wilderness areas and helping them discover the beauties of nature."

"That could still happen," Mandy said. "We can bring our kids there every summer for a few days."

He nodded. "Maybe that will happen then after all, right?"

"Of course it will! We want our kids to get to know and love you both," Mandy said.

"Also, Mom, how many of your friends actually have their grand-kids in the San Francisco area?" I asked.

She nodded. "Very few."

"That's what happens these days," I said. "We go wherever we can just to get a job. But you two know we love you both, don't you?"

They both nodded

"And every day we take with us all the lessons you've taught us through the years."

"It's just that this," my mom pointed at our choir, "is not what I dreamed for you as you were growing up."

"We're temple worthy, we try to live a good life, we love the Savior, and we try to treat others the way He taught. So that's all good, right?" Mandy said.

"Yes, that is the most important thing," her dad said.

My mom was embarrassed to be crying in public. "We're going to go to our hotel to rest up. Come get us after you're done here."

We hugged them both as they left.

"Well, that went well, right?" Mandy said with a smile.

"Yeah, I guess so. At least they understand what we're all about."

After the choir sang for its third and last time, we thanked them for their hard work and excellent concerts and then wished them a happy Fourth of July.

After the concert, we got our folks at their hotel and did a little more site seeing with them, including the construction site for the Philadelphia Temple. We also toured the Philadelphia Museum of Art which we all enjoyed.

By that time they were tired so we walked back to their hotel, gave them both big hugs, and then headed home ourselves.

There was some sadness though for both of us, knowing that our parents were both disappointed we hadn't turned out the way they would have preferred.

But we still loved them and they still loved us. I guess that's all that counts.

Our parents left the next day.

   *   *   *

On Thursday of the next week half an hour before Pathway began, someone knocked on the front door of the meetinghouse at 39th and Chestnut. We usually left the front door locked. People came in the side door. I was there to help my singers as they practiced.

Mandy saw the man and came to get me. "There's a guy at the front door."

We went together to the door. He was in his mid to late twenties and he had a stroller with a baby in it.

I opened the door. "Can we help you?"

"My woman left our baby with me for a few days and I don't have any money to buy food and other stuff for the baby so I was wondering if you could help me out with a few dollars."

I was worried about setting a precedent that would bring lots of people to the church asking for handouts. I thought that was a decision a bishop should make but he wasn't there.

I looked at Mandy for what she thought we should do. But she was mainly interested in the baby. She stepped outside and looked at the baby, who was sleeping. "It's a girl, right?" she asked.

"Yes."

"Oh, she's so beautiful! You must be very happy."

He smiled and nodded.

"Let me talk with my husband for a minute."

Inside with me, she asked, "What do you think we should do?"

"I'm worried that if we give him money, he'll just keep coming back."

She opened up the scriptures on her phone.

"This is from King Benjamin's address." She began to read starting with Mosiah 4:16-17: "'And also, ye yourselves will succor those that stand in need of your succor; ye will administer of your substance unto him that standeth in need; and ye will not suffer that the beggar putteth up his petition to you in vain, and turn him out to perish.'"

She stopped and looked at me. "I think we should help him get his baby girl what she needs."

"I wish the bishop were here," I said.

"Why? So you wouldn't have to make a decision? I don't recall King Benjamin saying, 'Get the bishop to decide things like this.' And even if the bishop decided that he shouldn't use fast offering funds to help him, he still might give something from his own pocket."

I thought about it. "Okay. How much should we give?"

"How about ten dollars?" she asked.

"Okay. I think I've got a five in my wallet," I said.

Mandy had some singles. We opened the door. I handed him the money.

"God bless you," he said, shaking my hand and then he left.

I'm still not sure if what he told us was even true except that he did have a baby with him.

I spent the next few days reading and re-reading the rest of King Benjamin's counsel to us on this subject.

I ended up grateful for what I'd learned from that experience.

About a week later on my way back from NYC where I'd been to Carnegie Hall making final arrangements for my choir to sing at a concert, I was in Penn Station heading for the train that would take me back to Philly. I saw what I assumed was a drunk lying on the floor. My first reaction had been predicted by King Benjamin in verses 17 and 18 from Mosiah 4: "Perhaps thou shalt say: The man has brought upon himself his misery; therefore I will stay my hand, and will not give him of my substance that he may not suffer, for his punishments are just– But I say unto you, O man, whosoever doeth this the same hath great cause to repent; and except he repenteth of that which he hath done he perisheth forever, and hath no interest in the kingdom of God. For behold, are we not all beggars? Do we not all depend upon the same Being, even God, for all the substance which we have, for both food and raiment, and for gold, and for silver, and for all the riches which we have of every kind...And now, if God, who has created you, on whom you are dependent for your lives, and for all that ye have and are, doth grant unto you whatsoever ye ask that is right, in faith, believing that ye shall receive, O then, how ye ought to impart of your substance that ye have one to another."

And so, even though my train was about to leave, I ran to McDonalds and bought this man a Happy Meal, and came back and put it near him so he'd see it when he woke up.

I couldn't wait to tell Mandy what I'd done.

*   *   *

On the last Friday in July I was invited to speak with one of the vice presidents of Boyer College. We met for lunch. He had a lot of nice things to say about my work with my choir and also my outreach activities associated with the "Stop an Op" program.

"We very much would like to have you continue with these programs," he said.

"Thank you. I'll do that."

"Also, we'd like to offer you a position as our outreach coordinator. It would only be part-time now, but after you've graduated, we'd like to make it full time."

He named the salary both before and after my graduation.

"That's very generous." I paused. "I do have plans though of someday singing with the Metropolitan Opera."

"Good for you! But even if you do, you probably won't be in every opera they do, so you could still work here and sing for them several times a year."

"That's probably true."

"We just don't want to lose the momentum you've established here in Philly."

"So in terms of the choir, right now I'd just do the same things I'm already doing, but be paid for it?"

"Yes. You might have to attend a few boring meetings with us but we'll try to keep that to a minimum."

"Let me call my wife and see what she says."

"Of course."

As soon as I left him, I called Mandy and told her of the offer. "What do you think?"

"I'm all for it! I want to call my dad and go, 'Guess what? My husband has a real job!'"

"Yeah, he'll be relieved."

I told her how much they were willing to pay me.

"You've got to be kidding! That's amazing!"

"I know."

We celebrated by going to the Manhattan Temple on Saturday.

The next week I met with the president of the college and asked if I could get an assistant to help run the "Stop an Op" program, someone who spoke Spanish if possible.

He asked if I had anyone in mind. I told him about Alejandro, how that he was the one who tried to hold me up but was now in an online college program. "When he finishes that, he plans on being a student here."

The president asked to meet him.

A few days later Alejandro met with the president and made an excellent impression, and a day later received an offer. He has been a great success in motivating those in minority groups to get more education.

Maria and Alejandro got their own apartment and a week or two later invited us over for dinner. Angelina showed Mandy her room and her toys and her princess dresses. Of course Mandy took great delight in it all.

After dinner, Alejandro had some grape juice for us to have a toast.

He had written down what he wanted to say. "To our good friends who bless our lives. We thank much."

We drank to that and then hugged each other.

As a special surprise, they had invited a quartet from the choir to come and sing for us.

That brought tears to our eyes and we hugged them all.

*　　　　　*　　　　　*

In late October as Mandy's due date approached, I was determined that I would be with her in the delivery room no matter what happened.

I turned down a request to fill in for someone again at the Met because, although it was still three weeks before her due date, I was not going to be gone again like I'd been on the day she had her miscarriage.

I called her twice a day at work to make sure she was doing okay.

When she had pains one Saturday, I wouldn't go grocery shopping because I didn't want to miss being there when she needed me.

"I'll be okay," she said. "Besides, we need groceries."

"We've still got some food."

She went to the kitchen. "Green beans, corn, two eggs, and three slices of bread."

"You know what? That's all I need for my famous corn-green bean-corn- egg sandwich."

"Face the truth, Davey Boy. The only thing you can cook is a peanut butter jelly sandwich, and for that you need four spoons and three knives. Why won't you go to the store?"

"I'm afraid you'll go into labor and I'll miss being there."

"Okay, look, go to the corner deli and get some things. You can be back in five minutes. I promise not to have my baby while you're gone."

"Okay, I'll hurry." I ran to the deli, grabbed as much stuff as I could, paid with my credit card and then ran back.

Mandy watched me put what I'd got in the fridge. "You got a frozen pizza for before we go to the hospital?"

"No, that's for me after you have the baby. For us now I got a hoagie. Oh, but also I got you broccoli salad. That's known to be really good for pregnant women."

"Says who?"

"The Broccoli Foundation of America."

She started laughing. ""You're too much, Davey Boy!"

The pains went away as we ate. I, of course, claimed it was because of the broccoli salad. Mandy threw a piece of broccoli at me and that started a broccoli war.

Finally the big day came. On Monday of the second week in November, I left our apartment about ten in the morning because I had a small group vocal class at eleven. Mandy was up but was having some labor pains, but she said I should go to work and that she'd call me if anything changed.

She called about two in the afternoon and told me to come home. I told the secretary I was leaving and asked her to let Professor Klein know where I'd gone.

Once I got back to our apartment, Mandy was ready and waiting for me. We took a cab to the hospital, filled out the paper work and were soon directed to the labor room, which was a room with several beds located near the delivery room.

There were already five other women in the labor room. A couple of them had been there all night.

"Well, we made it this far," Mandy said.

"Yeah, we did. What can I do for you?"

"Give me a priesthood blessing."

"Sure, I'd be glad to do that."

I stood up near the head of the bed, and opened my oil container on my key ring, put a few drops on Mandy's head and then placed my hands on her head.

"Excuse me. What are you doing?" a nurse called out.

"I'm going to say a prayer for my wife."

"What did you just pour on her head?" the nurse asked.

"Olive oil."

"I will have to speak to the doctor, but I can't do that now."

"Take your time." I placed my hands on Mandy's head.

"What are you doing now?"

"I'm going to ask God to bless her."

"Like I told you, I will need to talk to the doctor," the nurse said.

"You need to talk to the doctor in order for me to pray?"

"Go ahead and let him do it," another patient said. "It can't do any harm, right?"

"Go ask the doctor now," I said.

She glared at me and left the room.

While the nurse was gone, I gave Mandy a blessing.

"I'd like one of those too," the woman who'd stood up for us said.

By the time I was nearly finished with this other woman, the doctor and the nurse came in.

"What are you doing? This isn't even your wife," the nurse complained.

I closed my blessing.

"I was praying for this woman for when she had her baby."

"You're a Mormon, right?" the doctor asked.

"Yes, sir, I am."

He turned to the nurse. "It's okay. This is what they do." The doctor left.

Even though I knew that Mandy was close to having her baby I wanted to bear my testimony to these women. "When our Lord Jesus Christ was on the earth, he healed the sick. He gave that power to his apostles and it has been restored again to me and to many others."

"Yeah, right," one of the women scoffed. "That's what they all say. What proof do you have that what you're saying is true?"

At that time the nurse was checking the woman I'd just given a blessing to. "You're ready to go now," she said.

As they wheeled her out, the woman said, "You want proof? I was here all night and nothing happened. This guy prays over me and five minutes later I'm good to go. If that isn't God, then what is?"

"Could you pray for me too?" another woman asked.

I did and then said, "I need to tell you all that I am a member of the Church of Jesus Christ of Latter-day Saints. We believe in the Bible and the Book of Mormon. Oh, and we have a prophet too."

Mandy was the next one to go into the delivery room. I went in with her, although in retrospect, I should've stayed in the waiting room and read a magazine. I was not prepared for the effort and straining and pain involved in a woman having a baby. I never realized what a big deal having a baby is.

But finally it happened. Mandy had our baby, a beautiful baby girl with brown hair. I was especially pleased that she cried very loud.

"She's going to be good singer!" I thought.

*   *   *

Mandy stayed in the hospital one more day and then they released her. I was surprised they'd trust us with a newborn baby.

Normally a new mom's mother might come for a few days to help out, but Mandy didn't want her dad around, and she felt my mom would only make her feel incompetent, so we told our parents that we didn't need them, which meant we relied on ward members. If it hadn't been for the women in our ward, we'd have been in big trouble. These good sisters came and helped and kept coming, and we were very grateful for their kindness and knowledge about how to take care of a baby.

I was not much help. I could hold our baby but if she was crying I had no clue what to do to make her stop.

After a week though, we'd learned enough to get by.

We decided to call our baby Destiny. That was what we thought of the good she would do in her life, not so much because of fame, but because of her goodness, kindness, and love for others. We hoped that would be Destiny's destiny.

Three weeks later my mom and Mandy's dad came out for a visit. We couldn't put them in our apartment because there wasn't enough room so they stayed in a hotel not too far from our apartment. It wasn't that great of a hotel but it was within walking distance. Not that they walked though. They were afraid they'd be mugged if they walked, so they always took a taxi.

They stayed a week.

On Saturday when I was home, my mom kept busy doing what she called straightening up, which for her never ended.

Finally Mandy's dad had had enough. "Would you please stop what you're doing and just sit down and relax?" he asked.

"I'm just trying to straighten up things here."

"Did Mandy ask you to do what you're doing now?" Mandy's dad asked.

"No, but I'm just trying to help out."

"If she didn't ask you, then don't do it!" he grumbled.

"Why would you want me to stop?" my mom asked.

"Because Mandy is going to believe that you think she's incompetent if you keep doing this."

"This isn't just about Mandy, is it?" my mom asked him.

"No, truthfully it isn't. Back at the ranch, I've been putting up with it, but last week when you started to straighten up the barn, that was the last straw. It's a barn, for crying out loud! Just leave it alone!"

"What do you want me to do here?" my mom asked.

"I want you to go to Mandy and ask 'Is there anything I can do for you today?'"

"What if she says no?"

"Then don't do anything."

"But I came here to help out," my mom said.

"That's not true! You came to show her you love her and her new baby. That's the reason we both came. If you keep this up, you're going to put things away in places she'll never find. And, also, she's going to feel like you don't think she can do anything right."

My mom pursed her lips to keep from crying and went into the kitchen and started to make a cake from a cake mix.

While she was doing that, my dad went in to talk to Mandy.

A short time later my mom asked if she could talk to me in the kitchen.

"Do you need me to go to the store for you?" I asked.

"No, I need to ask you a question. When you were growing up, did I ever make you feel like you couldn't do anything right?"

"Mom, you were always an amazing mom for me."

"Thank you. I'm so grateful to hear you say that."

I held her in my arms and told her how much I loved her and also how grateful I was for the opportunities she'd given me and how, when I was growing up, I always knew she was there for me.

"Can you think of anytime when I made you feel like you couldn't do anything right?"

I paused. There were times but I wasn't sure if I should say anything.

"Please tell me," she said.

"Well, when I was in grade school, every Monday when I came home from school, you'd give me the clean clothes you'd washed for me and you'd tell me to put them in my drawers. And every week I'd put my socks in the first drawer, but every Tuesday when I came home from school, they'd be in my second drawer."

"That's because socks go in the second drawer," she said.

"Maybe to you they did, but not to me."

She sat down on a kitchen chair and grabbed a paper napkin and dabbed her eyes as she cried.

"It wasn't a big thing, Mom, and it didn't matter to me."

"I'm so sorry. All I ever wanted was to be a good mom to you."

"You were, Mom. You really were."

I sat down next to her at the table and hugged her. "I love you, Mom. I love you so much."

"I love you too, David."

I held her hand while she cried.

After a few minutes, she stood up and wiped her eyes. "Well, the good news is that I've learned something useful today."

"What, Mom?"

"There's a phrase I need to learn and I hope you'll remind me of it when I need to hear it. The phrase is, 'It doesn't matter.'"

"For many things, Mom, it really doesn't matter."

"How come I'm just learning this now?" she asked.

"That's the way life is, Mom. We're always learning new things."

She nodded. "I guess so."

Mandy's dad came in the kitchen. "Is that a cake baking that I smell?"

"It is. And I made it just for you," my mom said.

"That's great! And to show you what a good guy I am, I'll even share some of it."

"What a good person you are," she said with a smile.

"Why, thank you. Oh, I talked to Mandy. I told her you were going to come in in a few minutes and ask if there's anything you can do to help out. I suggested she come up with one or two things, but if not, you wouldn't do anything."

"What did she say?'"

"She didn't believe me at first, but I assured her that was what was going to happen. So after some thinking, she came up with three things you can do."

"Good."

Mandy's dad grabbed a book from our small bookshelf, opened it up and slipped a scrap of paper at about the halfway mark, then closed the book. He handed it to my mom.

"When you go in to see Mandy, take this book in with you and tell her how much you're enjoying it. That will put her at ease that you're not thinking she's the world's worst homemaker, but that you actually have a life that doesn't require you to rescue people from their lack of organization skills."

"That doesn't seem honest to me to say I'm reading a book when I'm not," my mom said.

"Then start reading. Read like the wind!"

"Read like the wind? That makes no sense."

"What can I say? I'm from Wyoming," he said with a big smile, and then he hugged her.

Things got more relaxed after that for all of us. The next day our folks bought two large history books about Philadelphia and spent their time reading them unless Mandy or I asked them for help. They also took short sight-seeing excursions around Philly.

After that both Mandy and I began to be more relaxed around my mom.

One day my mom asked if I would go with her to the Barnes Museum in Philadelphia which features post-impressionist and early modern art.

We saw paintings by Van Gogh, Matisse, Picasso, Renoir, Cezanne and Rousseau and many others.

"This is a dream come true to be here and see these masterpieces up close," she said. "Thank you so much for bringing me here. Your dad has no interest in things like this."

"Mom, he's not my dad."

"I'm sorry. Please forgive me."

"It's okay."

"To tell you the truth, "I said, "I'm not sure what to call him. I mean I could always go with step-dad, but that's a little awkward like as a greeting, like in the morning, when Mandy says, 'Hi, Dad.' I usually say, 'Hi there' or 'How's it going?'"

"Do you think you'll ever feel comfortable calling him dad?"

"I don't know. Maybe some time."

"He wishes he had a son. You're the closest he's ever going to get to that."

"That's true."

"Remember when he thought up a way for you to go on a ride with Mandy by having you upwind of the rest of us? Well, I asked him afterwards why he did that. And he told me that after he'd talked to you, he realized he needed to help you. I asked him why. And he said, 'Because he's temple worthy. That trumps a horse allergy any day.'"

My mom continued. "He did this for you because he wanted you to marry his daughter. Because he trusted that you would treat her well. You're not going to get any higher recommendation than that."

"Thank you for telling me."

"He's on your side and he always will be. Sometime when you feel good about the idea you might start calling him Dad. Take your time though."

"Okay, I'll work on that."

"Is there anything you'd like me to tell you about your real dad?" she asked.

"Like what?" I asked.

"Well, for one thing, I see a lot of him in you."

"You do? What?"

"The desire to achieve and aim high. He honored his priesthood as you do. Sometimes I see his smile in you. I'm sure he's very proud of the man you've become."

"I hope so." I sighed. "Mom, if Dad hadn't died, how would I be different now?"

"I have no way of knowing that. I'll tell you one thing though. I see so much good in you now. I don't think you'd be that much different than you are now. But of course we'll never know."

I gave her a big hug. "Thanks, Mom, for raising me."

"It was my great pleasure."

We ate in the museum cafeteria. We looked at all the other couples and tried to guess which ones actually loved art and which ones had been dragged there by a friend or loved one who did appreciate art.

It was a great time for my mom and me.

After that I did consider calling my step-dad "Dad" but I couldn't do it. To do so might be taken that I'd forgotten my real dad.

On fast Sunday in December our folks were there for the blessing of Destiny. Mandy's dad stood in the circle, along with our good friends in the ward..

Destiny slept through the blessing which was very considerate of her.

On Sunday after church, Mandy's dad and my mom asked if they could talk to us after dinner.

"We've heard you both tell about how it was almost miraculous the way you two met and fell in love in such a short time," my mom said. "We want to tell you that we feel the same way. First the Lord had to get you two together before he could get us together. We feel that the Lord had us in mind as well as you two, and we're very grateful to you both for our happiness."

Mandy leaned over to me and said softly, "That must mean that all the fireworks we experienced on our first time together was heaven-sent, and not just because I was amazingly hot!"

We both started laughing.

"You're still amazingly hot!" I said and then gave her a big hug.

The next day my mom took Mandy shopping for baby things. Her dad and I baby sat Destiny. They left just after Destiny had been fed, and after she'd fallen asleep. Not much happened. She did wake up after an hour. Mandy's dad picked her up and walked around the room until she fell asleep again. He kept her in his arms while we watched a game.

When Mandy and my mom returned, they were both in a good mood. Of course they had to show us everything they'd bought, which took a long time. They both seemed happy with their adventure and with each other as well. And that made me happy.

Later that evening, when Mandy and I were alone, she said, "I like your mom much more now than I used to. I think she's going to be a real good grandmother to our kids."

I nodded. "Yeah, I'm sure she will be."

Two days later our folks left, telling us often that they admired us for serving others here in Philly. We both knew that was hard for them to say, and we were grateful they'd said it.

*   *   *

Vladimir contacted me every few weeks reassuring me that they were looking forward to having me come up and be with them as soon as one of their tenors retired, which looked to be only a few weeks away.

We started to try to figure out where we'd like to live when we moved to NYC. One of the sopranos told me she and her family enjoyed living in Baldwin, Long Island, which was just an hour by train on the Long Island Railroad to Penn Station and then a subway ride to the Met. The advantage for her was there were houses with lawns and back yards so it wasn't like living in the City.

In mid-March Vladimir called and told me they were prepared to offer me a contract to be full time with the Metropolitan Opera, starting in one month. He faxed the contract to me that next day.

It was very generous. I showed it to Mandy and then asked her, "What do you think?"

"This is what you've always wanted."

The next day I submitted my resignation to Boyer College and told our landlord we'd be gone in a month. We decided to still serve in the Primary until we left.

The next weekend we drove to Baldwin, New York, had a real estate agent show us a bunch of houses and actually put an offer on one of them.

A few days later our offer was accepted by the owners of the house. It was going to be a great house but I worried about our being able to make the payments.

While we were there, Vladimir took us to lunch in the City. It was a very expensive and exclusive restaurant which had pictures of Broadway and opera stars.

While we were eating, Vladimir told me, "If you ever want to make a little extra money, on Sundays from noon to 8, they have singers come and sing. If you were to spend one Sunday a month, and just be there two hours, they would give you five hundred dollars. For two times a month that's a thousand dollars a month! And that doesn't even include the tips you'd get from the patrons."

"That might be good because of how high our mortgage payment might be," I said.

"So, are you interested?" he asked.

"Yes, of course."

Mandy shook her head. "In our church we don't normally work on Sundays," she said to Vladimir.

"Well, this isn't actually work," Vladimir said. "It's more like singing for friends. And it would help you with your mortgage payment."

"How can you even think of doing this on a Sunday?" Mandy said privately to me.

"I could do it after church," I said.

Our new ward meets at nine in the morning, but next year it will start at one o'clock and go to four. So how could you do it then?"

"Once or twice a month I'll just go to the earlier ward. It's no big deal."

"It's not just about church! We need some family time with you too."

"No problem!" Vladimir said with a big smile on his face. "Bring your family! You'll all get a free meal and meet some people who have an absolute love for opera."

Vladimir introduced us to Alexis Petrova, the manager, telling him about my recently filling in at short notice in the role of Rodolfo in *La Bohéme*.

"My wife and I were there that night! You did a great job! What a pleasure to meet you!"

"And this is my wife Mandy and our daughter Destiny."

"So good to meet you! Let me provide for you our most decadent dessert as my gift of friendship to you."

"Thank you so much."

"David is thinking he might come and sing here on Sundays once or twice a month," Vladimir said.

"Oh, that would be absolutely delightful! That would be such a wonderful thing for us, and, hopefully, for you as well."

The dessert was very good but Mandy wouldn't eat any of it.

On the way back, Mandy wouldn't even talk to me. But the next day she unloaded on me for even thinking of singing in a restaurant on a Sunday.

"Let me remind you," I began, "that the mortgage payment on the house we're buying is about two thousand dollars a month. Singing two Sundays a month would help a lot."

"So why are we buying such an expensive house?" she asked.

"I want you and Destiny to be in a decent neighborhood."

"And, of course, because you want to entertain your snooty new friends too, right?"

"And what is wrong with that?" I asked.

"I can't talk to you about this anymore."

"I'm only doing this for you."

She turned on me. "Oh, give me a break! You're doing it for yourself. What is happening to you? Do you even remember saying to me, 'If I ever value money instead of people, then you'll know that I'm on my way of becoming a selfish jerk.' Well, news flash, this is what I see happening to you right now*!*"

"It will all work out. You'll see."

A few days later our realtor called and said he was having a little difficulty getting our loan approved because I'd made so little over the past few years.

He explained. "I've told them that your new salary will more than allow you to make the payments. I'm confident it will be approved but it might take a few more days. I'll call you when that happens."

     *   *   *

At our next choir practice, I told our choir that we were leaving. We all ended up in tears.

When we got home, Mandy asked, "How can you do this?"

"It's not easy."

"I wish I thought that was the case for you but I don't."

On Saturday afternoon Mandy took a call from President Allen, our stake president, when I was out with Destiny. He asked if Mandy and I could meet with him at our ward meeting house.

She told him yes.

When I got home, she told us about our appointment.

"Why didn't you tell him we're moving in a month?"

"Because he's the stake president."

When we showed up for the appointment, the stake executive secretary met us in the hall. "President Allen is using the bishop's office today. He wants to speak to both of you."

He led us to the office and knocked on the door. President Allen opened the door, smiled and shook our hands. "Thank you so much for coming! Sorry to break up your Saturday. Oh, wow, your baby is so beautiful. What's her name?"

"Destiny. Oh, and thank you," Mandy said.

He had a daughter about the same age as Destiny, so we talked about that for a while, and then he said, "Well, the reason I needed to talk to you both is that after prayer and fasting we feel strongly that the Lord would like us to extend a call to you to be the bishop of your ward."

After a long painful silence, Mandy said to me. "Tell him."

"We're actually planning on moving to New York City in a few weeks. I will be singing with the Metropolitan Opera."

He stood up and shook my hand. "Congratulations! Look, I'm so sorry for wasting your time. We wish you the best! And thank you for being such a blessing to our stake."

We thanked him and left.

On our way to the bus stop we passed an old man. As we passed, he came up to me. "Can you spare a few dollars?" he asked me.

I lost my temper. "If I give you money, you'll just end up using it for whiskey or drugs! I'm so sick of this whole thing!" I stormed away.

Mandy, in tears, took both of his hands in hers. "I apologize for him. He doesn't mean it. He's just having a bad day."

He nodded. "The money is not for me. It's for my wife, for her medicine," he said softly.

"How much do you need?" she asked.

"Twenty dollars," he said. "I know that's a lot, but anything you can give will help."

Mandy nodded and found a twenty dollar bill in her purse. With tears in her eyes, she handed it to him.

"God bless you, Ma'am," the man said softly.

"You too," Mandy said softly. She wiped the tears from her cheeks.

"Is something wrong, Ma'am?" he asked.

She shook her head. "No, I'll be fine. Thank you for asking though."

The man shook her hand and left.

Mandy and I were facing each other, about ten feet apart. Tears were running down her cheeks.

"What is wrong with you?" I asked impatiently.

"'If I ever...'" She started and then stopped.

I knew where that came from. It was what I'd said to her when she told me she was worried that someday I'd become a selfish jerk.

I still remembered my reply to her. *If I ever ignore people who are having a hard time. If I ever think I'm too busy to help someone. If I ever turn down a calling. If I ever value money instead of people, then you'll know that I'm on my way to becoming a selfish jerk.*

I sighed. *It's happened*, I thought.

I wanted to hold her but I wasn't sure she'd even want that. "I'm sorry."

She nodded. "It doesn't really matter if you're sorry or not, does it? It's too late to turn this around. With our buying a much too expensive house, with you about to be surrounded by talented egotistical snobs, I have no hope for you to ever be the way you've been here. I have had such great respect for you here." She sighed. "You were my hero."

I feared the worse. "Are you going to leave me?" I asked.

"No."

"What will you do then?"

Destiny started fussing. Mandy picked her up and comforted her. "I will stay with you." She brought her hands to her face. "I'm sure the main thing you want to know is if I'll still go to bed with you. I will continue to do that because that is one of the duties of a wife. And of course I will take care of your kids, and cook and clean for you." She sighed. "My guess is that you'll be too busy to even notice any difference."

She took a deep breath. "So what I will do is...."

She shook her head. "I will just..." She sighed. "...lower my expectations."

I desperately tried to talk myself into thinking that once we got into our new home, she'd cheer up and enjoy our new life. I so much wanted to discount what she'd said. I wanted to blame it on her being a silly, emotional woman.

But I couldn't do that. I loved and respected her too much for that.

What if she's right? I thought. *If it's the wrong move for Mandy, how can it ever be the right move for me? More than anything else, she's the most important thing in my life. Am I willing to risk losing her respect? And what will happen to my relationship with the Lord if I walk away from an opportunity to serve Him? What does that tell Him about my priorities?*

"You're right! I can't let this happen! Let's go." I grabbed the stroller and turned to head back from where we'd come.

"Where are we going?" she asked.

"Back to the church!"

"Why?" she asked.

"To talk to President Allen."

"Why?"

"I need to accept the calling."

"How can we do that? We're buying a very expensive home in New York, and you've quit your job here, and you just signed with the Met."

"I'll get out of all that!"

"How are you going to do that?" she asked.

"I don't know, but I will."

"What about the Met?" Mandy asked.

"I'm not going to work there. I'm going to continue working at the college."

"But you just resigned from there."

"I'll redo that too."

"Why?"

I stopped and turned to face her. "I just realized that you're right. If I go to the Met, I'll become what you've always worried I'd become, a conceited, selfish jerk."

"But why are we going back to see President Allen? He's probably already called someone else," she said.

"I need to let him know we're staying here."

When we reached the church, President Allen was just leaving the meetinghouse.

"Can we talk to you again?" I asked, trying to catch my breath.

"Yes, of course."

He let us in and we all ended up in the office where we'd met with him before.

"President, I just realized that I've been going the wrong direction and I need to change that. I'm not suggesting you need to re-extend the call for me to be a bishop. You've probably got someone else in mind now, and that's fine. Regardless of that, I can't be in the Metropolitan Opera at this time because it will change me for the worse."

He sighed. "When you two left, I tried my best to think of someone else we could call. When I prayed about it, I had what can only be called a stupor of thought. So you can be certain that the Lord still very much wants you to serve in this calling. I've heard of the service you give to others in our ward, and also to the community through your choir. What we appreciate about you is that you reach out to others, no matter their situation in life."

I shook my head. "President, that's not me. That's Mandy. I've learned all this from her."

He nodded. "The same is true of me, and my counselors… and, actually, all the bishops in our stake. We have all been taught by our wives."

"President, I'm not sure I can be a bishop, but if you need a stake music chairman, I'm your man."

He laughed. "Nice try, but no cigar! Oh, sorry! I'm probably not supposed to say cigar here, right? Anyway, the way you feel now is the way I felt when I was called as stake president. But the thing I've learned is that the Holy Ghost can and will help you as you strive to serve those in your stewardship. Be worthy of that influence, and you'll do just fine. And, of course, you can always come to me or my counselors if you need some advice. I guess the only thing I need to know is if you will accept this calling from the Lord."

"Yes, I will."

Mandy reached over, smiled and squeezed my hand.

"Thank you so much. Now all we need you to do is tell us who you want to be your counselors. We'd like to do this tomorrow in Sacrament Meeting. So call me later today when you've reached a decision after making this a matter of prayer."

He turned to Mandy. "Since he doesn't have counselors, we'll have him use you as a counselor just for today as you talk about who the Lord wants as his counselors. And of course I'll need to talk to them before

Sacrament Meeting begins. Maybe even today, depending of course on when you reach a decision."

"I would be honored to help him with this, President," Mandy said.

"Thank you." He stood up and turned to me. "Do you have any questions for me at this time?"

"No."

He shook our hands and thanked us for our willingness to serve the Lord, and then escorted us to the door.

"Let's just focus on basic things for now," Mandy said.

"Like what?"

"Our baby needs her diaper to be changed, and I want you to do it."

"Okay."

I took Destiny into the men's room and changed her.

When I returned with Destiny, Mandy took her. "Not bad. I'm impressed."

We left the meetinghouse. I thought we were done and started toward where we needed to wait for our bus.

"Hey Bishop!" she called out loudly.

I shuddered and turned to face her.

"Do you know what makes me the most happy about your calling?" she asked.

"What?"

"You know something that very few people know."

"What's that?"

"'My Lord He has no throwaways.'"

I nodded. "It's true. He doesn't. I've learned that from you. I was forgetting that, but today you helped me get it back."

I sighed. "When I saw the expression on your face right after I'd yelled at that poor man who asked for some money, I knew I was heading the wrong direction. That's when I became so worried that you and I would end up not being as close as we've been, and also that I would lose God's approval if I continued going the direction I was going."

We sang our song while waiting for our bus.

The first thing I did when we got home was to call our real estate agent in Long Island.

"I'm so glad you called!" he said. "I was out of the office yesterday but today I saw that we received the letter indicating that they've approved your loan. Congratulations! I'll send you the papers today for you to sign."

"Actually I've changed my mind. We've decided to stay here in Philly. We won't be buying that house after all."

He swore at me and then hung up.

Next I called our landlord and told him we weren't going to leave our apartment after all.

"Glad to hear! You good people!"

Next I called Vladimir. He was furious that I was backing out on our agreement and told me to never think about ever being associated with the Met because that would never happen as long as he was there.

I also called the president of Boyer College at his home and told him I wasn't quitting after all. He said he was very happy to hear that.

Finally I called Alejandro and told him we would still be working with the choir. "Very good!" he called out.

Finally Mandy and I sat around at our kitchen table and talked about possible counselors but couldn't come to any conclusion.

"I think I'll call your dad," I said. "He's been a bishop before. He might have some advice for me." So I called.

He answered.

"This is David."

"David? How great to hear from you. How are things going?"

"Good, real good." I sighed.

"How's Destiny?"

"Growing up fast."

"I'm sure she is. We wish we lived closer so we could see her more often."

"That would be great." I sighed. "Actually I called because I need some advice from you."

"Okay, what's up?"

I took a deep breath. "I was just called to be a bishop of our ward, and I was hoping you could give me some advice about picking counselors."

"David was just called to be a bishop!" he announced to my mom. "He's asking me for some advice on how to pick his counselors."

"That is wonderful! We're so proud of you!" my mom said. "I'll let you two talk."

"Love you, Mom."

"I love you too, David! I can hardly wait to tell people in our ward about your new calling!"

Mandy's dad continued our conversation. "Well, this worked for me in picking my counselors. Pray first and then go through the ward roster until a name jumps out at you. Do that again for your other counselor and then you're done."

I paused. "What if a name doesn't jump out at me?"

"Do the whole process again."

"That's it?"

"Yeah, pretty much."

"Anything else I should know?" I asked.

"A new bishop might think his job is only to please the stake president, but the truth is your calling is to listen to the Spirit as you serve the members of your ward and follow the promptings you receive. Keep that in mind and you'll do fine. Your stake president will be happy to help you at any time, Also, if you ever want to run something by me, just give me a call." He paused. "Oh, by the way, I want you to know that I'm very proud of you."

I paused. "Thanks, Dad."

There was a long awkward silence and then he said softly. "You called me Dad."

"Yeah, I did. Is that okay?"

"Of course! It makes me very happy!"

"Me too. Do you want to talk to Mandy?"

"Not right now. You two have got enough to deal with right now. We'll call her on Sunday after church."

We said our goodbyes and then Mandy and I prayed and then went through the ward list until we had our names. And then we knelt down and prayed for confirmation. And then I called President Allen and told him who I wanted as counselors. He thanked me and asked me to be about a half hour early for church in the morning.

We got Destiny fed and diapered and laid her in her crib.

We sat on our couch. Mandy held me and told me over and over again that she loved me and she was confident that I was the right person for the calling and that she would do all she could to help me. That was the only thing that allowed me to get any sleep that night.

On Sunday we started a new adventure.

After being a bishop for six months, I can tell you from experience that there are no throwaways in our ward. Each one is precious to Father in Heaven and Jesus Christ. Also, there are no throwaways in the hundreds of people I see every day as I ride the bus to and from work.

So this is the foundation for everything I do now, and hopefully for everything I will ever do: My Lord He has no throwaways.

That's our song now and, hopefully, will be forever.

Made in United States
Troutdale, OR
02/01/2025